Paying the Price

FOR FOLLOWING JESUS IN PAKISTAN

Eva Wongsosemito

NEW HARBOR PRESS
RAPID CITY, SD

Copyright © 2024 by Eva Wongsosemito.

All rights reserved. No part of this publication may be reproduced, distributed or transmitted in any form or by any means, including photocopying, recording, or other electronic or mechanical methods, without the prior written permission of the publisher, except in the case of brief quotations embodied in critical reviews and certain other noncommercial uses permitted by copyright law. For permission requests, write to the publisher, addressed "Attention: Permissions Coordinator," at the address below.

Wongsosemito/New Harbor Press
1601 Mt Rushmore Rd, Ste 3288
Rapid City, SD 57701
https://NewHarborPress.com

This book is based on a true story. However, to protect the privacy and identities of the individuals involved, certain names, characters, places, and details have been altered. Any resemblance to actual persons, living or dead, events, or locales is coincidental. The essence and core events of the story are true, but some artistic liberties have been taken to ensure the anonymity of those involved.

Ordering Information:
Quantity sales. Special discounts are available on quantity purchases by corporations, associations, and others. For details, contact the "Special Sales Department" at the address above.

Paying the Price/Eva Wongsosemito. -- 1st ed.
ISBN 978-1-63357-455-7

*"For your sake we face death all day long;
we are considered as sheep to be slaughtered.*

But in all these things we are more than conquerors through him who loved us."

—Romans 8:36–37

I dedicate this book to all my brave brothers and sisters who have been persecuted, abused, imprisoned, tortured or died a martyr's death for Jesus' sake.

Acknowledgments

This book would never have been written if Salman Ahmed, the main character, had not confided his life story to me so candidly. During my stay in Pakistan, I often sat opposite him for hours, armed with pen and notebook, while he was telling his remarkable story. I could also ask my many questions. Salman, I thank you so much for those precious hours! You can be sure that your story will be a blessing and encouragement to many.

Semahoro, you were absolutely indispensable in the whole process. Ever since your personal meeting with Salman, you have spared no time or effort to obtain the Swedish edition of his life story and then you went looking for the author. Thanks to the Lord for this divine connection! From the very first moment we met, you were the driving force behind the creation of this book. Without your efforts and tireless dedication, this book would not be published. I would like to express my great appreciation and immense gratitude for your delightful cooperation and your passionate effort until the last moment!

My precious German friends, I'm not allowed to mention your names, but I am also very grateful that you agreed to translate this book into English. I really appreciate your coming forward with this offer of help! This not only saved me significant time and effort, but gave me the opportunity to work with a good English translation right away. You have made a significant contribution to the creation of this book. Thank you very much!

One person I certainly cannot forget to mention is my highly esteemed brother Paul Karkainen. What an incredible and time-consuming job you have done! Many hours of editing have finally resulted in an error-free, easily readable manuscript. Thank you so much for your gratifying collaboration with a particularly beautiful result. Your love for Jesus and the expansion of His kingdom has often deeply touched me.

With respect and admiration, I would also like to thank Paul Estabrooks for his efforts and very useful advice to make my book even more beautiful. You have devoted extensive time to give my book "The Finishing Touch." Magnificent! Thank you for your wonderful ideas! I feel very honored that a man like you were involved in the publication of my book in the USA.

Finally, I would like to thank my dearest husband and my precious children and grandchildren for their help and support throughout the whole process of writing and everything that came with it. I'm so grateful to have you all in my life! Your loving support and interest have encouraged me again and again. I feel truly blessed!

Eva Wongsosemito

Endorsements

Only one word can express my impressions after reading this book. **Riveting!** Since I had briefly met Salman before, I thought I knew his story. Few of us in the Western world can truly identify with the pressures of life that Christians like Salman experience in Pakistan and other countries of Christian persecution. But his perseverance and the faithfulness of God shine brightly through those cloudy skies. It is so encouraging to know Salman is still persisting in his evangelistic efforts. This book is a **must read** for anyone who does not follow Jesus, or who claims to be a disciple of Jesus.

Paul Estabrooks
author of *Night of a Million Miracles*

The story about Salman is a true story. I first met him when he was one of my students in the mountains of Pakistan. When I gave the students an exam in the end of my teaching, Salman got the highest score. His dedication for the Lord was obvious. Later on I met him many times, sometimes as one of the leaders in the Bible School but also when he was married. He continues to bravely serve the Lord in a nation where the majority only recognizes Jesus as a respected prophet. Pray that this mass of people will see the true identity of the risen Lord!

Josef
Missionary, Sweden

Eva Wongsosemito's Paying the Price illuminates the incredible strength of those who courageously follow Jesus amid intense persecution in Pakistan. As an Iranian who has also journeyed from Islam to faith in Christ and serves Iran's underground church movement, I found this book deeply moving in its portrayal of the resilience and sacrifice required to walk with Jesus. It is a powerful testament to the unwavering faith of believers who persevere in the face of adversity. I highly recommend this book to all Sunday Christians in safe countries—it offers a profound understanding of the depth of commitment among persecuted Christians.

Dariush Golbaghi
Founder, Safehouse Ministries

My wife and I met Salman **before** reading his life story. We were impressed with his focused love for our Lord Jesus Christ. His biography expands our understanding of his life and passion to serve Christ...without fear. Through disciples like Salman, we can be assured: Jesus is in Pakistan!

James (Jim) Cunningham Ed.D.
Founder of Go Teach Global Society

EVA WONGSOSEMITO

Salman Ahmed's story is a riveting account of a life transformed by the power of the Gospel. As a South African, I have experienced how difficult it can be to share the Gospel with Muslims in my own country. Yet Paying the Price portrays how much higher the cost is for those who, like Salman, live in areas where following Jesus can cost one's very life. Salman's faith is a persevering faith in the face of virulent opposition. I highly recommend Eva Wongsosemito's eye-opening book. It has personally challenged me to engage more proactively in sharing the Gospel, and in supporting and praying for fellow believers who lay down their lives daily for the One who gave His own life to redeem ours.

Dr. Avril van der Merwe
Author, Pastor

I feel very honored to write an endorsement for your new book. I have only read some chapters and can already taste the inspiring effect on my personal faith experiences from the first pages. I am convinced that this book will be a great blessing to many.

> Pastor Antoon Sisal
> Paramaribo, Suriname

Salman's courageous journey is a shining example of the transformative power of faith and the unwavering pursuit of the Way, the Truth and the Life. In the face of persecution and adversity, his conviction and resilience inspire us to stand firm in our faith. His story underscores the profound impact of love, forgiveness and acceptance in Christ. May Salman's testimony ignite hearts and minds, and spark a chain reaction of hope, love and redemption. This book is a must-read for everyone!

> Semahoro

EVA WONGSOSEMITO

Contents

Preface 1

Introduction 7

In Search of the Truth 15

My First Christmas 29

Honor Killing 35

The Escape 47

The Unknown City 55

Survival 63

Testing 73

Training 81

Outreach 95

Calling 103

Mistrust and Discrimination 111

Persecution 117

Nowhere to Stay 123

On the Run Again 129

Future Prospects 135

Six Years Later 143
Postscript 161
About the Author 165

Preface

Dr. Naji Abi-Hashem, Lebanese American, Clinical & Cultural Psychologist, Author & Speaker, Independent Scholar, and Associate with Member Care International

Significant *Religious Conversions* and profound *Spiritual-Experiences* are clearly a vivid example of the active role of Faith and the genuine place of Spirit, as they constitute the true substance of our humanity and the central agency of our true beings.

Such deep *Transformations*, on the mental, emotional, habitual, spiritual, and existential levels, are strong evidence of the power of the Gospel of Jesus Christ, which is the dynamic divine influence that is constantly moving behind the scenes, touching our essence in significant ways. This penetrating effect of the Holy Spirit is still at work today, as it has been in the past and will continue to do so in the future, transforming people "inside-out," transcending history in amazing ways, and intervening in personal lives and social affairs across time, culture, and space.

For those coming from different faith-traditions (mainstream religions), or pseudo faith-combinations (new-age movements) or even no faith-traditions (agnosticism, atheism) – to be able to miraculously discover the *Light* and fully embrace the *Christian Faith* is not a superficial matter or intellectual exercise, nor it is a mere sentimental thrill. Rather, such transformations constitute an authentic encounter with the Almighty, a full recovery of people's *Imago Dei* imprinted in them, and a restoration of the true faculties of their personality.

Vibrant conversions and lively spiritual experiences affect the deep core of the *mind, soul, heart, psyche, conscience*, and *will* of any human being. The evidence of its genuineness and the validity of its impact are manifested in a new surge of significance, a new vibrant attitude, and a new peaceful confidence, all of which soon begin to propagate to close friends, family members, and the community-at-large. Such authentic, satisfying, transforming, enduring, and resilient *Faith* is undoubtedly powerful and ultimately contagious!

Another *evidence* of authentic spiritual-re-generations and soul-renewals is manifested in the steadfastness displayed by these new *believers*, even when they think they are totally *alone* and no-other-like-them does exist in the country or whole world...

Also, their genuine *conversion* is tested and confirmed by their brave courage and resolved willingness to endure trials, mistreatments, oppositions, punishments, and persecutions, alone or together with like-minded believers. In their struggles, steadfastness, and suffering they provide a remarkable testimony to the Lord and the power of His Gospel (*Injeel in Arabic*), as their new faith keeps growing and shining brighter than gold. I personally have witnessed such a precious phenomenon firsthand in my home country and among many cultural groups and communities around the world (*Job 23:10 & Proverbs 4:18*).

The moving story of this book is challenging, inspiring, humbling, and refreshing. It makes us keenly aware of the unsung "heroes of faith" who are thriving elsewhere in the kingdom of God. They are behind the scenes, far away from the media lights, carefully and wisely conducting themselves in their social contexts and communal settings (*Matthew 10:16*). However, they remain very active, highly dedicated, and greatly beloved by our Lord.

Such stories of supernatural journeys and spiritual transformations also prompt us to fervently continue to *pray and intercede* for those believers, as our faithful brothers and sisters who are vital *members* of Christ's invisible and universal church. They live, work, and witness in tightly closed communities and very restricted countries, passionately carrying the *Cross of Christ* and boldly engaging in interfaith dialogue and cross-cultural outreach, evangelism, discipleship--across religious lines and worldview mentalities.

We certainly learn from them the beauty of endurance, the cost of discipleship, the reward of hardship, and the joy of faithfulness. Indeed, great is the mystery that "Christ in You is the Hope of Glory" (*Colossians 1:27*).

Soli Deo Gloria!
Naji Abi-Hashem, PhD
Seattle, Washington, USA & Beirut, Lebanon
September 2024

Introduction

While staying with friends in Pakistan, there was a sudden knock on the door. It was a young man from the neighborhood looking for me. He was a friendly nineteen-year-old student, who not long ago passed his final college prep exam. "I have come for prayer," he said candidly. We found a quiet place in the small living room, where there were a few plastic chairs. I invited him to sit and took a seat in front of him.

"Are you going to university now to continue your studies?" I asked. "Yes, I did originally plan to," he replied. "But in the meantime, God has called me to do missionary work. That is why I've come to you. Would you please pray with me? I want to reach people who have never heard the gospel before." He told me about his plans and where he would go with his team.

"Young man," I said, "do you know that this is one of the most dangerous areas of Pakistan?"

"Yes, I know that," he replied. I looked straight into his young, shining eyes and said, "You are so young! **Do you know, this could cost you your life?**"

With palpable passion in his voice he replied, **"Yes, I know!"**

"And yet you want to go?" I asked respectfully.

"Yes, I want to go, because Jesus has called me." He exuded determination but also enthusiasm as he repeated his request to me, "Will you please pray with me!"

With reverent admiration, I laid my hands on this dedicated young man to convey God's special blessing on him in the name of Jesus.

I addressed God Almighty in a powerful prayer for protection for this young life, but also for the courage and strength to make disciples for Jesus in this so-dangerous region. And then he left. The door closed behind him. His brief visit left a deep impression on me.

Why is it that many Christians in Pakistan are willing to pay such a high PRICE to follow Jesus? Why is it that Christians in Pakistan attend their church every Sunday, while imposing security guards with loaded automatic weapons stand at the entrance of their church to protect them from attacks? If you go to church in Pakistan, you do not know if you will return home alive. And yet they still attend! Their churches are full!

A young Christian in a leadership position put it this way, "Here, we live in fear every day. Because in my country something can happen to us as Christians at any time. According to the constitution, we are allowed to preach the gospel and practice our religion," this young man said. "The vast majority of the population, however, is not happy about that. One can very easily make up false charges here and harass Christians on that basis."

"For example, one day I took a beating from the Military Police on the false charge that I had stolen something. After that, they kept me in custody for a long time. But I knew that the real reason was something completely different. I had handed out Bibles in a certain area and they did not like that." He continued, "Once, when my team and I showed a film about Jesus in a remote region, it almost cost me my life!"

The title and subject of this book is about the price Christians in Pakistan often must pay, if they really want to follow Jesus.

This makes me want to thank with reverence and awe our Savior and Lord, Jesus Christ, from the depths of my heart, that He paid the greatest *"Price"* of all when He died on the cross at Calvary for our sins. *"Thank You, Lord, that You paid this price, even for me!"*

When we talk about the Christians in Pakistan, the first thing to remember is that Pakistan is an Islamic republic with a population of over two hundred and thirty million. The percentage of Christians who live in this country is generally estimated at one percent, which means that there are more than two million Christians living in Pakistan.

It is certainly not my intention or the intention of the main character of this book to hold anyone accountable for events that describe the difficult position of Christians in this country. I consider myself blessed that during my visits to Pakistan I met very fine people, including Muslims, who treat Christians as equal human beings. I enjoyed their tremendous hospitality and count them among my friends. We mutually respect one another.

But Pakistan is as it is! And Christians often pay a high price if they want to follow in the footsteps of Jesus, the Messiah. An even higher price if a Muslim takes it into his head and heart to become a Christian!

One day I visited a Christian family. I saw a man sitting in their living room, in a white robe, clearly dressed as a Muslim clergyman. While my hostess was busy preparing tea, I struck up a conversation with this man. He told me that he was born a Muslim but had recently started following Jesus. He talked about the Christian meetings and Bible studies that he attended and found so beneficial. I asked him if his family was aware of this. "No," he replied.

"And if your family finds out about this?" I inquired sympathetically. After some thought, he replied, "Yes, that will probably happen one day. And frankly, I am afraid . . . very afraid . . . !" I prayed with him, knowing it could cost him his life. He knew it too!

During many conversations with Pakistani Christians, I kept asking myself, "Where do all these people find the courage?" One young active Christian put it this way, "I think when God calls us in a country like this and gives us a ministry, He also equips us with *courage* and *boldness*." And this young man knew what he was talking about! He himself had been a victim of violence, intimidation, and deprivation of liberty on several occasions. Contact with these courageous Christians became **"life-changing"** for me.

This book tells an exciting and true story. During many interviews, the main character in this story vividly described his remarkable experiences. Deeply impressed and encouraged by those who know him, I decided to write this story and share it with the world. In order not to endanger the people in this story, I have used fictitious names.

Eva Wongsosemito
January 2019

• CHAPTER 1 •

In Search of the Truth

MY NAME IS SALMAN Ahmed. When my search began, I was nineteen years of age, a strict believing Muslim and extremely proud of that. I was also convinced that I already had extensive knowledge of everything important about Islam. And I had only one great desire, which was to become an *Imam,* a spiritual leader. So, I could be found in the mosque every day for my training on becoming an Imam.

Among other things, I was learning Arabic so that I could study and understand the Quran in its original language. Furthermore, I had also begun to learn Farsi, the language spoken in modern-day Iran. In fact, many books about Islam were written in this language. In addition, I was trying to memorize as many chapters of the Quran as possible, because a good Imam is supposed to be able to quote the Quran by heart. My parents were extremely proud of me.

During this time, I also learned to hate Christians. My parents instilled in me as a little boy at home not to have contact with Christians. They told me Christians were bad people who adhered to wrong teachings and served idols. They also told me the Christians' spiritual book, the Bible, was corrupted. Because of this and various other stories, my mind formed a very negative image of Christians.

From my childhood, I could well remember the times when Christians came to work as street sweepers in our neighborhood. It was often 45 degrees Celsius in the shade. If you had to work in the sun, you also had to drink copiously, otherwise you ran the risk of dropping dead in the street. When their supply of water ran out, they would come and ask us for water. Because we had learned to hate Christians, we gave them water, not in a glass or cup, but in used dirty plastic bags or other dirty containers. Thus, I had grown up with a deep dislike for Christians, and that dislike was intensified by my studies. I really began to hate Christians!

Throughout my education, my teachers always hammered home that we should never, ever read the Bible. It was a strictly forbidden book for Muslims and certainly for a future Imam. Thus, I had only negative thoughts about the Bible and became convinced that it was a bad book.

But, on the other hand, it also made me curious. I sometimes thought, *"Why does everyone around me hate this book?"* I really wanted to know the reason for this and why the book was forbidden to us. My curiosity began to grow and, one day, I made a secret agreement with myself, "If I ever find this book somewhere or am offered it by someone, I will take it and read it. Because I want to find out what is so special about this book and what the reason could be that this is a forbidden book for us."

But I did not have access to a Bible! So, I continued reading daily from our holy book, the Quran. I also read other books, which helped me further in understanding the teachings of Islam. During that time, I often visited a store where you could buy unbelievably cheap secondhand books. I was especially interested in books on Islamic history, the history of my country Pakistan, world history, and just about anything that could expand my field of vision.

One day I was browsing in this little store again. A somewhat smaller book suddenly caught my attention. I picked it up and read the inscription on the front page: *Injeel Muqaddas*, which in English means "The New Testament," or literally translated, "Holy Scripture."

Wow! I thought this must be part of the Bible, the book about which my teachers made such a fuss. Although, as a student of Islam, I was strictly forbidden to ever touch this book, let alone read it, curiosity tempted me. I looked around to see if anyone was watching and quickly hid the booklet under my long white robe. After all, I could not actually buy it! It was a forbidden book for me, and no one should know that I had it in my possession. I checked out the other books of my choice at the cash register and left the store.

I always sought out lonely places to read my dubious acquisition. Sometimes I even did it in the middle of the night when everyone was asleep. To read in the dark, I used the small light of my cell phone. I had to be extremely careful not to be caught by anyone. While reading, many questions came to mind. I marveled at the statements Jesus made about Himself. Three statements aroused my interest:

1. ***"Very truly I tell you, whoever hears my word and believes him who sent me has eternal life and will not be judged but has crossed over from death to life"***—John 5:24

2. ***"Can any of you prove me guilty of sin?"***—in John 8:46

3. ***"Jesus answered, 'I am the way and the truth and the life'"***—in John 14:6

In my circles, everyone said that the Bible was corrupted and, therefore, a bad book, which you should not read. But I found important news in it; namely, if you accepted Jesus, you were safe, you were saved. And **He was the way**.

So, with these discoveries, I made the naïve decision to go to one of my teachers, a very knowledgeable Imam, who might be able to give me more clarity. But, instead of an answer, he attacked me in a stern voice: "Surely you know that the Bible is an evil and corrupted book! Why did you start reading it *anyway*?" I said to him, "Teacher, I just wanted to know what it says!"

My overwhelmed teacher apparently had no answer and I was given a punitive measure instead. To make matters worse, he also threatened to tell my parents that I had been reading and studying the forbidden book. Frankly, that was the last thing I needed! And my questions were still not answered.

I had no idea where I found the courage, but my curiosity was so great that I asked another teacher a few days later, hoping that he could give me a sensible answer. To my surprise, he responded even more vehemently and demolished me with his words. Then, for days, I was psychologically torpedoed and emotionally abused, tortured, and bullied by my teachers through the ugly words and curses that they hurled at me. But again, alas, no answers!

I concluded I was wrong to ask these questions from my spiritual leaders. I would have to find out for myself! So I decided to read the New Testament a second time. Maybe I would find an answer in it. Again, I carefully began reading in secret. And again, it took a long time. This time, however, I discovered something new. "Jesus Christ came into this world because of **our sins**. Yes, he **died** for our sins." I thought to myself, so then He also died for **me** and **my sins!** The Quran teaches that if I sin, Allah will **punish** me for it. The Bible says that Jesus bore my **punishment**. All kinds of thoughts began to run through my head and made me increasingly restless.

I could no longer go to anyone with my questions. I would have to find out everything for myself. I started reading and studying the Quran again. I wanted to know if the Prophet Muhammad also made such statements about himself. I wanted to know if he also said somewhere, that if we believed in him, Prophet Muhammad, he would save us and that he **knew** where we would go then, that he **knew** about the way to heaven. Maybe I had overlooked something.

And this time I found a clear answer. The Bible told me that Jesus was **without sin**. The Quran, however, said something completely different about the prophet Muhammad. It really dismayed me! In the 48th chapter, in Quran verses 1–2, I came across a conversation between Allah and Muhammad, where it talks about Muhammad's sins and forgiveness for them. In Al-Fath 48:2, I read, "So that Allah may forgive you for your past and future shortcomings, perfect His favor upon you, guide you along the Straight Path."

I was amazed! Muslims thought that all prophets were holy. But then, why did Allah speak of forgiveness? Jesus Christ said of Himself, "*Can any of you prove me guilty of sin?*"—in John 8:46. Here I found my first answer. As I compared the New Testament to the Quran for the third time, I came across the verse that would completely change my life. Jesus said, "*I am the way and the truth and the life*"—in John 14:6.

I wanted to clarify for myself whether Muhammad could save me or not. Thus, I took another in-depth look at the Quran and came across the following statement of Muhammad in chapter 46, verse 9. Here, the prophet answered questions of his followers about what would happen to them in the future: **"Nor do I know what will happen to me or you."** Again, this statement upset me profoundly! The following thought occurred to me, *"As God's prophet, surely he should know these things?"*

After reading this verse, I worryingly asked myself if all my efforts to be a faithful Muslim were perhaps in vain? Were we as faithful Muslims perhaps losing our whole lives by following the Prophet Muhammad? After all, the Quran stated that Muhammad said that he did not know what would happen to him nor what would happen to us. I found this discovery to be **very shocking!**

I concluded that, as a faithful follower of the Prophet Muhammad, I had no assurance of my salvation. I discovered that I may have wasted all my time on something that gave me no certainty, no security after death. I knew my body would die one day, but what would happen to my immortal soul? Was I perhaps following the wrong man?

Again, I came across John 5:24 in the forbidden book, where Jesus said, "***Very truly I tell you, whoever hears my word and believes him who sent me has eternal life and will not be judged but has crossed over from death to life.***"

I suddenly realized that Jesus was the only one who could save my soul. **"I didn't want to be lost!"** So, I decided to accept Jesus Christ. For He knew the way! He had the power to save me! He came into this world to bear the punishment for my sins in my place. He was the only one who could remove God's judgment on me!

As I searched for the right words, I began to pray, "Jesus, You are the only one who can save my soul! . . . You are real! . . . I believe in You . . . Apart from You, there is no one who can save me. You died for my sins and for that I thank You. I now accept You as my Savior. From now on I want to follow and serve You!"

Suddenly, inexplicably, a deep inner peace filled my heart, a peace I had never known before. I felt extremely happy for the first time in my life. It was a very special experience, in which I felt God's nearness intensely. And at that moment the thought came to me, "I was lost, but now I am found! I was spiritually blind, but now I can see!" Later, this became one of my favorite songs:

> *"Amazing GRACE, how sweet the sound,*
>
> *That saved a wretch like me.*
>
> *I once was lost but now am found,*
>
> *Was blind, but now I see."*

Now that I had converted to Jesus, I wanted contact with other Christians. I had no idea how to pray and honor the Lord. I needed to find a Christian church!

One day in our neighborhood, I saw a woman at work. She was sweeping the street. By her clothing I suspected she was a Christian. I saw that there was no one around who could hear me. I spoke to her and said that I would like to meet her pastor. She spontaneously invited me to attend a Sunday service at her church and gave me the address. I could hardly wait to go there the next Sunday and to participate in the church service.

It was a totally new, but also a very special experience for me. After the service, I asked the pastor if I could talk to him, and he really took time for me. I told him in detail about my search and how I found the Bible. I also told him how, after studying, researching, and comparing the Bible with the Quran for a long time, I came to the conclusion that I was following the wrong person.

The pastor was extremely interested and listening closely. I then told him of my decision to follow Jesus. I also shared with him the moment that I prayed to Jesus and accepted him as my Savior, and that I now wanted to learn to live as a Christian.

The pastor believed my remarkable story and accepted me as a new believer. This was not a given. Christians in Pakistan were often afraid of a "Muslim" visiting their church. I could well be a spy posing as a Christian, preparing an attack on their church. But I had been accepted here and attended church services every Sunday from that day on. My faith was strengthened by this worship and fellowship, and I enjoyed it immensely.

CHAPTER 2

My First Christmas

IT HAD BEEN ABOUT three months since I invited Jesus Christ to come into my life. My parents did not yet know about my conversion and that I was secretly attending a church. I always had to camouflage things well. I just used the clothes I always wore when I was still in training to become an Imam, a Muslim spiritual leader. I still had the same beard of a "Muslim cleric in training."

I was afraid of what my parents would do to me the day they discovered that I had become a Christian. I had every reason to be afraid and to even consider the worst as Muslims could be very cruel if a family member made a rash decision to become a Christian. But I did not want to think about this right now. It was Christmas, **my first Christmas!** I had joy and peace in my heart and knew that I had eternal life. No one could take that away from me!

Meanwhile, I had the opportunity to meet all kinds of Christian friends, not only from my church but also from other churches. The day, when all Christians celebrate Christmas to commemorate the birth of Jesus, had come. I was very curious about it and a group of friends from a Catholic church had taken me there to witness the celebration of Christmas.

I took off my shoes at one of the entrances to this large church, as was the custom in my country, and placed them among all the other shoes already there. I then reverently entered the church and took my place among the other visitors while my friends were still outside. Everything I saw and heard fascinated me.

Suddenly, I felt a hand on my shoulder. I turned and stared at the stern face of someone in uniform. "Come with me!" he ordered. Startled, I stood up and followed him. He turned out to be a security guard. It was quite normal in Pakistan to hire armed guards for larger gatherings and certainly for crowded church services. Yes, it had even been made mandatory by the government, to prevent attacks against Christians as much as possible.

My dress and appearance were Muslim, and this apparently made him suspicious. He asked me in a threatening tone, "Who are you? What did you come here to do?"

I answered, "I am a Christian and have come to attend the Christmas service." Soon I found myself surrounded by more men in uniform, all from security.

They did not believe me and snarled, "Show me your ID!" Trembling with fear, I pulled my ID card from my pocket, knowing that it would state I was Muslim. That made things even more difficult for me! A loaded gun was pressed to my temple.

In desperation, I told them I had friends there who could confirm I was a Christian. The guards finally allowed me to call them on my cell phone. To make matters worse, my "friends" did not feel like coming in. They were outside drinking and partying with other friends, while I was experiencing anxious moments and fearing for my life! I finally managed to convince one of them of the urgency of my situation. He came in and declared, "Yes, I know him. He is my friend, and he is a Christian." Unfortunately, that did not help either.

Still holding the gun to my temple, they ordered me to leave the church building immediately. They pushed me toward the exit and said, "Run! Otherwise, we'll shoot you!" My hands grasped my long robe, and I ran out of the church in my bare feet. And I kept running, running for my life! Without looking back, I just kept running, as far away from this place as possible. My shoes were at another exit of the church, not that I would ever go back there.

A safe distance away, I looked for a *rickshaw*, a kind of covered moped cab, to take me home for a small fee. During the ride, disturbing thoughts crossed my mind. Satan began to speak to me, "See, you are not really accepted! Because you are a converted Muslim, they treat you differently! You will always be a stranger among Christians!" I occupied my mind with these negative and depressing thoughts for a while longer.

And then suddenly, I heard inside me the voice of the Holy Spirit quoting a Bible verse from Hebrews 12:2: "***fixing our eyes on Jesus, the pioneer and perfecter of faith.***" God's Holy Spirit began to speak to me, "Let go of those negative thoughts! Look to Jesus! Look to Jesus!" The moment I set my gaze on Jesus, peace and tranquility came into my inner being and vastly different thoughts came to mind. Even though Christians refuse to accept me, that does not change my position before God. I am still a Christian, a beloved child of God, bought and paid for by the blood of Jesus.

I would face more rejection because of my "Muslim background," even by Christians! But, apparently, that was all part of following Jesus. He too was rejected. But I could still follow in His footsteps.

CHAPTER 3

Honor Killing

WHAT I COMPLETELY FAILED to notice was that family members had been following me at a distance for several Sundays. Thus, they discovered that I secretly attended a Christian church every Sunday. One day, upon returning home, they confronted me about this. They let their indignation and disgust run wild with abusive words and slurs aimed at me.

But what particularly frightened me was the threat that they would kill me if any one of them saw me attending a church again or in the presence of a Christian. "You will bring shame and loss of face to all our relatives, our neighbors, and friends," they declared. I saw desperation but also hatred in their faces. I knew they would carry out their threats and would be able to kill me in a very cruel way if they caught me.

I was totally freaked out about it! What should I do? Should I give up my faith in Jesus Christ and go back to Islam? Should I resume my training as an Imam? No, a thousand times no! This was not an option for me!

Days and even weeks passed. I stayed at home and prayed to Him who forgave all my sins and absolved me from God's judgment and eternal damnation. I prayed to Jesus Christ, who loved me so much that He gave His life for me, dying on the cross. And as I secretly read my Bible each day, there was a growing realization that I could not really **follow** Jesus in this way.

Moreover, my parents would force me to go to the mosque with them again and resume my training as an Imam. I also missed the fellowship with my Christian brothers and sisters and the encouraging meetings in the church, singing those beautiful songs together, the worship, and the proclamation of God's Word. *"How can I go on living without this?"*

I was overwhelmed by all kinds of feelings. Feelings of fear and despair, but also feelings of courage and surrender to the Lord. In the end, the desire in me won, not only to **believe** in Jesus Christ but also to **follow** Him. It was the Holy Spirit of God who made room in my heart for my decision. Jesus Christ and faith in Him was too precious to me! There was nothing in this world for which I would be willing to give this up! And if this was the price I had to pay for following Jesus, then I was willing to give my life for Him!

I seriously considered that, if I now sought out Christians again and went to my church, I would probably have to pay for this with my life. But my reasoning was this: *They can only kill my body. No one can take eternal life away from me!* And I know that Jesus will be waiting for me to receive my spirit if it should come to that.

Tomorrow is Sunday and I will go! I will be there again together with my brothers and sisters. I will praise my Savior and Lord! I will be where I am supposed to be no matter the consequences. I am willing to die for Jesus because I will then meet my beloved Savior in heaven and be with Him forever!

Indeed, it did not take too long for my parents and relatives to discover that I was again in contact with Christians and attending church services. And they made good on their threats! One day, very early in the morning, I woke up to the screams of my father and other male relatives living with us. Fear overwhelmed me when I opened my eyes and saw the furious faces of the men, armed with iron rods, invading my bedroom.

But strangely enough, there was also a supernatural peace inside me. I felt the nearness of Jesus! Swearing and cursing, they shouted, "We are going to kill you! Today you are going to die! Your last hour has come!"

They cursed me loudly as they beat me mercilessly with powerful blows. I felt tremendous pain! I felt my bones breaking! As they yelled, "Have you come into this world to commit treason against our prophet Muhammad? Better you had never been born!" They then directed heavy blows at my face and head! Slowly I lost consciousness, believing that I was now going to heaven.

* * *

I heard sounds and voices very far away, which gradually became clearer. Very slowly my consciousness returned, and I discovered that I was not in heaven, but in a hospital. I was on a drip and could hardly move. Both my arms were in plaster and there were tight bandages all over my body. Even my head and face were completely covered with bandages. I was told that the bandages covered numerous stitches on my crushed face and that I had quite a head wound. I felt pain all over!

What happened? And how long ago? Slowly the memory of tremendous torture came back to me. However, the realization that Jesus suffered much more for me filled my heart with a supernatural peace, despite the terrible memories that kept recurring in my mind. *"Oh, thank You, Lord Jesus!"*

My mother visited me and told me that the men had left after beating me, thinking I was dead. She took me to the hospital while I was unconscious and covered with blood. Upon arrival, she told them that I was hit by a car.

No one would ever charge these men with attempted murder! Just as no one would come to my aid or call the police. This case was about *"honor killing,"* an unwritten law, often practiced in my country, where in most cases the perpetrators escaped punishment for murder.

For me, a long time of recovery and rehabilitation followed. I could never cease to marvel at the fact that I could still see with both eyes. I had no explanation for it other than that Jesus held His hands over my eyes during the extreme violence. My nose bone was partially shattered, and I had stitches just above and below my eyes and above one of my eyebrows. Yet my eyes remained fully functional. It was a miracle from God! And thanks to God's protection, my brain had not suffered any serious injury either.

During my hospital stay, a particularly nice nurse often came to my bedside to care for me. She told me at one point that she was a Christian. After some hesitation, I confided in her that I was also a Christian and believed in Jesus. One day, when no one else was around, she gently said to me, "Tell me honestly, you were not hit by a car, were you? Feel free to tell me the truth. What happened to you?"

I briefly told her, and she was very understanding. I felt that she was sent by God. She asked me if there was anything she could do for me. After some thought, I gave her the phone number of my pastor, which fortunately I could still remember. I asked her to call and inform him of my situation. And she did. She also told the pastor that I was not safe here and would need help to escape undetected. We had frequent contact with each other, and I owed her much. She was like an angel sent by God especially for me. But before I could think about a possible flight, I needed to recover and rehabilitate.

* * *

My body's healing process took many months! Walking required great effort because of the pain from all the bruises and damage I had sustained. Since both my arms were still completely encased in plaster, I was utterly dependent on the help of others. After being discharged from the hospital, my mother was the only one who looked after me and helped me. She lovingly cared for me despite everything, which gave me fond memories of her after her untimely death.

My father and my uncle were keeping quiet for now because they thought I had learned my lesson and chosen to believe in Islam again and would return to the mosque with them as soon as I was able. But they did not look after me. I still felt their hate towards me.

What they did not know nor understand was that, through my conversion, I became a new creation, a follower of Jesus Christ, with absolutely no intention of returning to Islam. They did not know that the power of the Most High God dwelled in me through His Holy Spirit. They smashed my body, but mentally I felt extremely strong and filled with the power of God.

I also cannot fail to praise the skill of the Pakistani doctors who treated my broken bones. Both of my elbows were broken, and these were extremely complicated fractures. But after a time of "cast off and cast on again," over and over, I could now use both my elbows normally again. As far as my face was concerned, the doctors also did excellent work in restoring me to a healthy, normal appearance.

The hair that was shaved to treat the head wound also grew back after some time, making me happy to look in the mirror again and say to myself, "You are still a fine-looking young man, a wonderful creation of God!" Yes, God was genuinely good! Thanks be to Him, but also to all the doctors and nurses!

Every time I thought about how they broke me down like this because I **followed Jesus**, my inner being filled with joy and a feeling of happiness. I felt no resentment towards my family but was grateful to be alive and allowed to endure all this for the sake of Jesus, who suffered infinitely more for me, granting me complete salvation. All the pain of rejection and disappointment I brought to my Lord. There was a constant supernatural calm within me that no one could take away from me.

Because of my extensive injuries, my body was forever scarred. My spirit, however, was whole and strong because of Jesus Christ, who lived in me. He watched over my soul and spirit so that they could not be damaged. I wear the scars on my body with reverent pride in honor of Jesus Christ, my precious Savior.

• CHAPTER 4 •

The Escape

ONCE I HAD REASONABLY recovered, my family warned me again, "The day we catch you meeting Christians, or attending a Christian church, will be your last! We will kill you!"

But I could not last very long, lacking fellowship with other people of faith. Moreover, I could not and would not continue to live as a "lonely Christian" in secret. So, I found a safe place and called my pastor. I asked him if he would be willing to meet me for a conversation at a restaurant far away from the church. "I must not be seen around the church! You know what happened to me. The nurse from the hospital has already told you about it."

The pastor agreed to my request and we set a time and place. I ended the conversation with: "Okay, pastor, I will wait for you there, but please come!"

"I promise! I will definitely come!" I heard him say. "Don't worry!"

A few days later, we met at the agreed-upon restaurant near us. No one knew him here and no one knew that he was a pastor. Thus, I could go to the restaurant with reasonable peace of mind. I told my family that I was going to meet one of my "former teachers" there. Which was not a lie! He was indeed my first teacher in the Christian faith.

We found a quiet place where we were not directly in the line of sight of other people. I then told him in detail about everything I had been through and what my family had done to me because I followed Jesus. My pastor could not hold back his tears upon hearing my story. He sincerely sympathized with me and tried to comfort and encourage me. He said, "Don't be worried! We, as a church, will do all we can to find a solution for you." We drank tea together and then I returned home. I would just have to wait.

* * *

Two weeks later, my pastor called me again and said that he had discussed my circumstances with the members of his church and that they were praying intensely for me. "If you want, we can send you to another city," was his suggestion. "Far from here, where you will be safe from your family." I said I would think about it. That was quite a decision to make! For the next few days, I considered it day and night in my thoughts and prayers. I had never been away from home before! But I also knew that if I stayed home, they would one day kill me anyway.

The realization slowly dawned on me that I had no other choice to survive. I would have to leave my home and my family if I intended to continue living. So, I decided to accept my pastor's offer. I went for a walk around the neighborhood so no one could eavesdrop and called him. I said to him, "Pastor, I am ready! Please help me!"

"Of course, we will help you!" I heard him say on the other end. "Get ready!"

A few days later, I received a call from the pastor. He told me about a fine Christian friend in another big city far from here. "I talked to him about you, and he said to me, 'Feel free to send that young man to us! We will take care of him and help him further with everything he needs.'"

Then he asked me, "Are you ready to leave?" I said, "Okay, give me a few more days because I need to figure out a way to disappear undetected and without a trace."

A few days later, I received the message that my train trip was booked and that I must be at the station on time. "I will meet you there," said my pastor.

On that day, I told my family I was going to visit the mosque. They had no issues with that. My God ensured that no suspicion would arise in them. They just let me go.

So, I left with nothing but the clothes on my body, my phone, and some pocket money worth about 2 euros. I could not take anything else with me. I walked in the direction of the mosque and then passed it, called my pastor, and told him I was on my way.

He responded with: "Hurry up! I am already waiting for you!" I paced myself and finally arrived at the station well ahead of time. We still had thirty minutes before the train would depart. My pastor handed me the train ticket for the lengthy journey, paid for by the members of his church. The pastor had also brought a bag of clothes for me and some extra money. He would inform his friend as soon as I was on my way, letting him know when to expect me. "I am sure he will take good care of you," my pastor concluded.

Finally, he prayed for me. He blessed me and said that the Lord **would open doors for me.** It was an emotional moment and we both cried. I was now fully aware that, for the first time in my life, I was about to leave not only my home and my family but also all my friends and the city where I grew up.

The train was already there, and it was time to board. My pastor hugged me and said, "Our prayers will be with you! Be blessed!" I took my seat on the train with my few possessions, which all fit into one small bag. The train slowly started moving, taking me to an unknown future.

During the long journey I clearly felt the presence of God. At times, a few tears rolled down my cheeks, but this time tears of gratitude and a deep awareness of divine safety. I knew I had made the right choice. I left home for the sake of my Lord and Savior Jesus Christ. To be able to follow Him and preserve my own safety, it was the right decision. The

Holy Spirit of God would guide me and be with me everywhere.

• CHAPTER 5 •

The Unknown City

Encouraged by my pastor's words and prayers, I spent the first hours of the long train journey with a sense of peace and gratitude in my heart. But as the hours passed, reality increasingly intruded on my thoughts. Feelings of immense sorrow flooded my heart. The realization that I was rejected by my own parents and family and that they wished me dead left feelings of deep pain within me. These feelings of pain, rejection, and disappointment increasingly dominated as the beautiful Pakistani landscape glided by. I missed most of it.

My thoughts were on everything I left behind in my beloved and familiar city of birth. Not only did I have to leave behind my parents, my three older sisters and other relatives, but also all my friends. My school friends, my cricket friends, my new Christian friends. Yes, I had to leave behind my entire world as I had experienced it, and that without being able to say goodbye! I would never see them again! Tears came and I could not stop them. Nor did I want to hold them back! I put a large cloth over my head and face, so that other travelers could not see, and I let my grief run unrestrained for a while. But then suddenly I heard that encouraging voice of Jesus again, speaking to me from deep within my heart, "My son, you gave up all this to follow Me! This is the price you must pay for choosing Me! But stay strong! I will always be with you and surround you with My love."

I now became aware that I had embarked on a journey where the final destination was still unclear. I felt a bit like Abraham, who was instructed by God to leave his country without knowing where he was going. All he had was the promise that God would show him the land. Similarly, I was now on a train heading for a totally unknown future. In a few hours I would arrive in a place utterly foreign to me. I had no idea of what awaited me there. I would have to seek the address of a Christian brother, who would take me in temporarily. *"Lord, I will need Your help and Your guidance"* was my silent prayer.

After many hours, the train reached the big city. All the passengers gathered their baggage and departed. I did the same, but without much baggage. The bag my pastor gave me was all I possessed. With the address on a piece of paper in my hand, I looked for a rickshaw to take me to a family who were strangers to me. During the nearly hour-long ride, I wondered where I would end up. This city was so different from my birth city, frighteningly different! And worst of all, they spoke a different language here, which I did not understand at all.

The official language in Pakistan was Urdu and I spoke that too. Furthermore, I could also speak the native language of the region where I came from. But here they spoke a different language, a language incomprehensible to me. I felt like a stranger in a foreign land.

After an hour, the rickshaw driver stopped and pointed in the direction of a house, the address where I had requested to go. I paid him the small fee and was welcomed by Brother Irfan and his wife. They had two children, a three-year-old boy and a baby girl. The house was tiny, but they were willing to share with me what they had. They showed me their bathroom, a cubicle with a hole in the stone floor where the water could drain out. There I saw a giant bucket, which held as much as twenty or even thirty liters of water, and an aluminum saucepan to scoop water from the big bucket. It felt wonderfully refreshing to use the cool water to rinse off all the dust and sweat from the long journey and to put on clean clothes. Squatting on the floor, I immediately washed the clothes I wore and hung them on a rope apparently put up for this purpose in the bathroom.

Refreshed and with clean clothes on my body, I was served a hot meal. It consisted of rice, a spicy soup of yellow peas, and roti. *Roti* is a kind of pancake made of flour, water, and a raising agent, fried on an iron plate. Our conversation was in Urdu, but they normally spoke their native language with each other and their children. I would also have to learn this language.

After dinner, they showed me the place where I could rest and sleep after my long and tiring journey. There was only one bedroom, where they slept together with their children on a large bed. There was a thin, narrow mattress on the floor next to their bed which was meant for me. These lovely people were apparently willing to share everything with me. For the first time in my life, I was introduced to the love and hospitality of Christians. This made a deep impression on me.

After several hours of sleep, I felt refreshed. It was around six in the afternoon and it was already starting to cool down a little. My host suggested we take a walk and learn about life in their big city. The narrow streets were teeming with people. But the walk became almost an ordeal for me. This city was much more modern than where I came from. In this Christian neighborhood, I found the clothing of some young girls quite shocking. I had great difficulty dealing with it. After all, I came from a Muslim community, where all the women, including the young girls, were completely covered, many even in burkas. Here, some girls walked around in tight jeans and airy blouses! I had a tough time dealing with this and, as a young man of twenty, I did not know where to look!

I was new to the Christian faith and wanted to live a life committed to the Lord! I did not want any temptations in my life! I shared this while walking with my host and he said to me, "Don't fix your eyes on the girls! Look into your heart! Do you see Jesus there? He says to you, 'I am your companion and walk with you in *My purity and My holiness.*'"

So, I focused on "Jesus in me" and it did indeed help. My God was mighty and saw into my heart. But I had to constantly refocus my eyes on Jesus and practice this. I would have to learn to deal with this. After all, I could not walk the city streets blindfolded.

In the evening, we sat together for a long time, giving me the opportunity to tell my story. It was past midnight when we lay down to sleep, my host, his wife, the two little ones, and I, all together in the same room. I could not fall asleep until the early morning hours, because I still suffered from the trauma of "reexperiencing memories." But I was also thankful that I was allowed to suffer for the Lord and that he miraculously spared my life. God must have a special purpose for my life. I was curious about His plans. And it was with these thoughts that I finally fell asleep.

• CHAPTER 6 •

Survival

THE NEXT MORNING, BROTHER Irfan's wife lovingly provided breakfast, consisting of a bowl of Pakistani tea, freshly baked *chapatti,* a special kind of roti, with fried eggs. After this shared meal, I thanked Brother Irfan and his wife for their loving welcome to their home. *"But what next?"* was my question.

Because of the cramped space, I understood that I would not be able to stay here for long. "I do want to rent a small room," I told him. "I have some money that my church gave me. Could you possibly help me find a place to live that is affordable?"

"Yes, I certainly want to help" was his reply. We brought this matter to our Lord in prayer and then we left the house to start our search.

My host knew many people in this neighborhood. We visited houses here and there to obtain information. Finally, we found a small empty room for rent that I could move into that same day. I paid and was given the key. "Mission accomplished," we concluded with satisfaction.

But I also needed a job to meet my basic needs and pay the monthly rent. God was so good! My skill in embroidery with beads and sequins, which I acquired as a young teenager after school, could possibly come in handy now. I shared all this with Brother Irfan on the way back to his home. It had become quite hot on the dusty streets of the city and our stomachs told us that it was time for lunch. While we were gone, Brother Irfan's thoughtful wife had prepared a large pan of spicy fried rice with pieces of potato in it to satisfy our hunger.

Later in the afternoon, a close family friend came to visit. He had heard that I was looking for work. When I told him of my ability in embroidery with beads and sequins, he had an idea. "I know someone who works in the garment industry. He has his own studio. Maybe he could use some help." Meanwhile, Brother Irfan's wife placed a plate of diced watermelon on the table, and we all enjoyed this wonderfully refreshing fruit. After talking some more, the friend said goodbye and left. He promised to contact the owner of the clothing studio. He would stop by again the next day.

On the following day, when we left my host's small home a little later in the afternoon, the narrow streets were already teeming with people. All the stores were open, and people were busy trading or shopping. Shakeel, my host's friend, had made an appointment for us over the phone to visit the studio in question. We made our way through the crowd of walkers, children playing, and street vendors. Occasionally, we saw how children marked out a piece of dusty ground to play cricket, an extremely popular sport in Pakistan for both young and old.

After some searching, we found a moped cab which quickly transported us to the other side of town for a low price. A brisk ride through heavy traffic took us to the right address. Shakeel paid the driver, and we entered the studio, where you could see at a glance that diligent work took place. The person accompanying me introduced me to the boss, who would hopefully give me a job. Our visit to this address proved not to be in vain. Through the mediation of my new friend Shakeel, the boss offered me a job and said I could start the very next day. Yes, God was indescribably good to me!

Returning to my host family, I enthusiastically told them I had found work and could start the following day. Together we thanked our Almighty Lord for all the prosperity with which He had blessed us over the past two days. It was time for the evening meal. My hostess placed a bowl of freshly cooked white rice on the table as well as a large bowl of spicy soup, with pieces of potato and beef in it and, of course, the inevitable chapatti as an accompaniment.

After the meal, I thanked the couple profusely for so kindly taking me in and being helpful in finding me a place to live. The time had come for me to pack my personal belongings and make my way to my new home. I would have to rise early the following morning to be at work on time.

Clients visited the studio daily with clothes that needed to be embellished with sequins and beads in all colors. This was typical of the clothing of dressier Pakistani women. My job was to first create an attractive design. If the customer agreed, I would then start working. Fortunately, I enjoyed my work.

My boss also conducted classes in this trade. After being employed for a while, he allowed me to support him during classes and help students become proficient in this trade. My boss seemed to be satisfied with my performance.

The working days were long though, and the pay was low. I spent the following months literally just surviving! I worked from 8 a.m. to 8 p.m., earning 200 rupees a day. That was about two euros and not enough for food. But by God's gracious provision, my boss provided me with a meal once a day at work. The rent for my sleeping quarters was 1,000 rupees (10 euros) per month. On top of that there were daily travel expenses to and from my workplace. I was still grateful, however, to have this job.

For the time being, I slept on the bare floor in the small empty room which I rented, with only a sheet under me. There were no cooking facilities either. But thankfully, I could buy a simple meal very cheaply at a food stall.

There I bought food twice a day for 50 cents per serving in a plastic bag. It certainly could not be called luxurious at that low price, but it filled my hungry stomach.

Only on Sundays could I attend church services and have fellowship with other Christians. I thoroughly enjoyed this. However, even in my simple living space, I could have daily contact with my Lord and Savior who meant so much to me. Again and again, I felt His peace flowing into my heart as I worshipped Him.

The days, weeks, and months crept by at a snail's pace. After deducting the rent, my travel expenses, and my daily food, I was left with exactly 500 rupees (5 euros). I put that aside every month. By living like this, I finally managed to save enough money for a mattress. It felt much more comfortable than the hard floor. I then started saving for a fan, as the heat was stifling in Pakistan for much of the year, often well over 40 degrees Celsius. Eventually. I was able to save enough money to purchase other necessities, such as a small table and two chairs as well as a pillow and blanket for the cooler time of year. Slowly, life in my little room was becoming a little more pleasant.

My life here consisted mostly of working, praying, eating, and a few hours of sleep. But I managed to survive this way. My "wealth" consisted of the privilege of following Jesus and knowing that He was constantly with me and in me. His unconditional love surrounded me. I felt blessed despite the difficult circumstances.

However, I would so like to have more contact with Christians and attend more meetings! I still knew so little about the Christian faith. I would like to learn much more about becoming a better Christian. So, I talked to my God about this, and He saw my desire. He moved my employer to give me a small daily wage increase after several months. By my calculation, this should allow me to make ends meet even if I only worked four days a week. My employer was also a Christian and understood my decision.

For example, I could now participate in activities at my church on Thursdays and Saturdays. I attended the Bible studies and prayer meetings. I could now also participate in the youth seminars, which were usually held on Saturdays. I was finally beginning to grow in my new faith.

• CHAPTER 7 •

Testing

THE FACT THAT I would now have more time for the Christian education I much needed pleased me enormously. I enjoyed the Bible studies and communal prayers. I also participated enthusiastically in the various seminars, which were always held on Saturdays.

But what I enjoyed most were the youth evenings, where young people of my age shared God's Word and their personal experiences with Him. We often formed smaller groups to talk about the topic at hand and to pray together and praise God for all the wonderful things He was doing in our lives. We also had a time of worship with the whole group, where the youth played various musical instruments. There was considerable variety in the organization of the youth meetings that sometimes included a "picnic" somewhere in a nature setting. Every now and then we also had sporting activities. I was actively involved when it included cricket, because playing cricket was really my thing!

But we also actively engaged in outreach. To share the gospel with people, or encourage them in their faith, we traveled to other places, including outside the city. We visited people in their homes and held "house meetings" for families and their neighbors. There we gave testimonies and shared God's Word with them.

At first, I tagged along just to learn, but after a while I also tentatively ventured to teach God's Word. Thus, I gained my first experience in proclaiming the gospel. All these activities gave more life to my previously rather monotonous existence. I felt incredibly happy.

***

A particularly memorable moment for me was my baptism. It was a festive occasion. Dressed in white, thirty people entered our church to be baptized by immersion based on their faith in Jesus Christ as their Savior. I was one of them. After my baptism, a feeling of intense happiness overwhelmed me. Now I was a *real* Christian! I belonged and since that day I have been a full church member with a Christian name which I received at my baptism. From now on I would go through life as Matthew Nadeem. This gave me limited protection and made it harder for the people who were after me to find me. All the brothers and sisters welcomed me, and I was now known to everybody. As a result, I was often invited to visit people's homes and to participate in their home meetings. It was a richly rewarding time for me.

***

One day, one of my friends came up to me after the church service asking if I would be willing to let someone stay with me. I was told he was a good Christian and a man of prayer. He did have work but did not earn enough to rent his own home. This is why they asked if he could live with me for the time being, in order to have a roof over his head. Of course I wanted to help, so I took him from the church to my humble place of residence.

We had quite an enjoyable time together. Every evening when I came home from work, we would have a time of prayer together. Since Dildar often arrived home from work earlier than me, I gave him a key to my apartment. And so we comfortably lived together for a while, managing quite well. But then Dildar suddenly lost his job and stayed at home alone for days. That was why the door was always open when I came home.

One evening I returned from work to find the door locked. I thought that maybe Dildar had to go somewhere or he found an evening job. So, I quickly searched for my own key in my pocket. When I opened the door, I was jolted by the fright of my life! Totally shocked, I could hardly believe what I saw! My house was completely empty! Everything was gone! Everything that I had managed to acquire, piece by piece, with hard work and living very frugally. It was all gone! I was devastated.

Distraught, I sat down on the bare floor and looked up at the empty walls. *"What should I do? Lord, my God, what should I do? This really cannot be from You, Lord. This is the devil's work!"* Anger arose within me. I grabbed the phone and called the friend who had asked me to take in this man. In my frustration, I reproached him on this matter. "How could you say to me that Dildar is a good guy? He emptied my whole house, probably sold everything to make money. Then he locked the door and left. I have nothing left, nothing at all! He even took my toothpaste!"

My friend was as shocked as I was and just said, "I'll be right with you." As I sat on the bare floor with my knees raised waiting for him, I literally was at my wit's end. My head and heart were filled with thoughts definitely launched by the devil. *"Now you've seen what Christians are like! This 'good boy' was a Christian, wasn't he? Look what he did to you! Don't ever trust a Christian again! They are all liars and thieves! You left your family and all your friends to follow Jesus. And your reward is being robbed by Christians! You can now see that you can't trust them, right?"*

But because of the Holy Spirit, who came into my heart on the day I received Jesus, my inner being soon ran out of space for such negative thoughts. He reminded me of the Bible passage in Hebrews 12:2, **"Let us keep our eyes fixed on Jesus, the pioneer and perfecter of our faith. For the joy set before him he endured the cross, scorning its shame, and sat down at the right hand of the throne of God."**

Perfect peace flowed into my heart! It was undoubtedly the voice of Jesus speaking to me. *"My son, do not look at other Christians, look at Me!"* This was so real and at the same time supernatural, a miraculous experience for me. I had nothing in my room, but my heart was filled with utter peace. God did not change my situation, but He touched my heart.

As I waited for my friend to arrive, I prayed to my God. "Lord, I remember reading a promise in Your book, the Bible, where You say that if we seek Your Kingdom first, You will give us everything we need. Lord, You are going to provide everything I need! I trust You and I will continue to serve You no matter what."

There was a knock on the door and, yes, it was my friend. He stood there with a large shopping bag in his hand. I let him in. He expressed his regret for everything Dildar had done to me and the trouble he had caused me. He opened the bag and took out a pillow, a sheet, and a warm blanket, because wintertime had begun. He also removed a drinking glass and two plates from the bag as well as shampoo, soap, toothpaste, and a towel. He said it was a gift from his family.

We prayed together and again expressed our trust that the Lord would provide for all our needs. Then my friend left. I folded the sheet in half and placed it on the floor along with the pillow. I then wrapped myself in the warm blanket my friend had given me and lay down. With God's supernatural peace still in my heart, I fell asleep within minutes.

• CHAPTER 8 •

Training

I WOKE UP IN the early morning and rubbed my eyes. It felt like a bad dream, but it was actually a harsh reality. My house was empty! None of my beautiful things were left in it. But I had to move on! I had to go to work, just like all the days before.

Quickly, I freshened up and dressed. After a short prayer, I locked the door behind me with a new padlock, which I had acquired somewhere nearby the night before. I stopped at the food court, where I had a standing order for two meals a day. I picked up my first meal for the day to prevent having to work on an empty stomach. Then I caught the bus to the studio, where I was now a regular employee.

Of course, upon arrival, I briefly told my boss of my shocking experience. He listened with understanding and compassion. But then work called and we moved on to the order of the day. I no longer felt the need to buy fancy stuff ever again! For the time being, I was going to save the money I had left over every month. Life continued as usual: long workdays, church attendance, youth evenings, and occasional outreach activities.

* * *

One day, a friend told me an intriguing story about a Bible school high in the mountains of Pakistan. He thought that a place like that would be beneficial for me, as I would learn to know the Lord much better there. Also, I could learn much more about the Bible and life as a Christian. He talked about it so enthusiastically that he piqued my interest. He told me there was little time to think about it, as the education and training of the next group of students would start within four days.

I wanted to pray about this first and ask the Lord if this was His will and plan for me. Furthermore, I also wanted to ask my pastor and my youth leader for advice. And I was curious what my other Christian friends would think about it. So, I took the matter in hand and approached them! To my surprise, they all responded positively and encouraged me to go.

But there was another fundamental problem. The school was in a different region, a long way from here. I would first have to travel by bus to another city. Upon arrival I would have to take another bus, which would transport me high up in the mountains to my destination. The little money I had set aside amounted to nothing and was certainly not enough to cover the travel expenses, let alone the school fees, including board and lodging. For me that was a huge amount! I discussed this problem with my God and asked Him to provide if that was where He wanted me to be.

At work, I also informed my boss about my desire to go to Bible school. He would have to give me time off for the next six months. I also carefully shared my financial problems with him because that was the reason why it was not yet certain that I would be able to go. After coming home from work, I would pray about this matter again and ask the Lord for His special favor and guidance.

Suddenly my phone rang. It was my boss, also a devout Christian. He asked me if I could quickly come to his office. *"Of course, boss"* was my answer and I immediately set off. Once there, my employer handed me 2,000 rupees and said, "Go and take that training! This is enough to start with. I wish you God's blessing and a wonderful time!" I thanked him profusely for his gift and joyfully made my way home, thanking and praising the Lord in my heart. I considered this a confirmation from God that I may go. My pastor gave me an additional 1,000 rupees.

Meanwhile, I had also received an official invitation from the leadership of the Bible school, in which they informed me that I could come and would be warmly welcomed. Now I could leave. I had no idea what I would find there, so I packed everything I thought I would need, including my pillow, sheet, and blanket.

Full of excitement, I sat in the bus on the way to an unknown future. After several hours in the overcrowded bus, we reached our first destination. Upon arrival, I stepped off and looked for the stands of the buses traveling in all directions. Looking around, I could already see the high mountains which appeared blue gray at this distance. After some searching, I found the right bus and continued my journey.

I had never been to the mountains before, so I feasted my eyes on them in amazement. One magnificent panorama after another revealed itself to me. But, as the bus climbed steadily higher, I began to feel increasingly miserable. The higher we rose, the more "hairpin bends" the bus had to take before climbing along the steep cliffs. Clearly, I could not handle that very well. I was glad when the ride was over.

I had no idea that it would be so much colder than in the valley and I had no warm clothes with me. The other students benevolently shared theirs with me, which made me feel right at home with them. It was like one big family, even though we did not know one another. We were some 2,300 meters above sea level here, something I had never thought about. No wonder the temperature here was so much cooler than in the valley. The air was a bit thinner as well, but wonderfully clean.

I had yet to fill out my application form. Since I decided to participate in this training at the last minute, there was no time to do it beforehand, as was usual. Then another student showed me to my room, which I would share with a few other students during our studies. We introduced ourselves and decided on sleeping places. I made my bed with the sheet, pillow, and blanket that I brought with me. I put the rest of my things in the cabinet provided.

After dinner, we all made our way to the hall where classes were normally held. That evening it was the location of our "Introduction Night." There were twenty-three students and thirteen staff members, consisting of some teachers, a cook, and several others. The students came from all parts of Pakistan. We formed a large circle so we could see each other well. It was a blessed evening, where we not only learned about each other, but also heard many testimonies of God's guidance and His financial provisions.

As the school was self-sufficient and did not hire staff, everyone had to do their bit. The staff divided the work among the students, so everyone knew what was expected of him or her. My first practical task for the next few weeks was to clean all eight *"washrooms"* (toilet and shower) daily. As I had thirty minutes to complete this task, it was a race against the clock every day. My next task was keeping everything neat and tidy outside the building for the period of a month. Finally, the staff assigned me to dishwashing duty for the entire remaining time. Since we often had guest teachers, washing dishes for an average of forty people was quite a job, which two of us had to do manually.

We had a tight daily schedule. Every morning, we rose at 6:00 a.m. for a personal quiet time with God until 7:00 a.m. Then we had thirty minutes to freshen up and dress for the day. The staff served breakfast at 7:30 a.m. Those who showed up too late received punishment in the form of extra work. Alternatively, the latecomer had to do push-ups. As being on time was quite a problem for Pakistanis, this disciplinary action proved a necessity. Students performed household chores from 8:30 to 9:00 a.m. followed by communal worship and prayer from 9:00 to 10:00 a.m. During that time, students also took turns in providing short reflections. Each morning, three students were given five minutes each of speaking time. In this way, we were a blessing to one another and at the same time practicing public speaking.

Morning classes lasted from 10:00 a.m. to 1:00 p.m. with a short tea break in-between. From 1:00 to 2:00 p.m. there was time for a communal hot lunch followed by an hour of rest. The afternoon program began at 3:00 p.m. We would then form groups of five or six students with two leaders each for Bible study and prayer. An hour and a half later, our sports program began. Because we were eighteen boys and five girls, most of the games were cricket or soccer, but sometimes another sport. The sports were voluntary though. I always participated in cricket games. At 6:00 p.m. we had to return to the classroom, refreshed and wearing clean clothes. The lessons with frequent interaction lasted until 8:00 p.m. After this, the staff served dinner. From 8:45 to 9:30 p.m. was *"worship-time"* (praise and worship), accompanied by those who could play musical instruments. We followed this daily program Monday through Friday.

Saturday and Sunday were free days. Saturdays were usually for washing clothes and cleaning rooms. For the remainder of the day, we could do whatever we wanted. There was always the option of playing sports and on Sundays we always attended a service with the whole group at a local church, which was a twenty-five-minute walk away. We always enjoyed this. The sun shone most of the time at this high altitude with beautiful views along the way.

These church visits led me to become acquainted with a boy who had a bookstand next to the church. He sold Christian reading materials, CDs, DVDs, and other Christian items. Many tourists passed by there, most of whom were Muslims. And there were always curious ones among them who would buy something. This boy's bookstand piqued my interest, and we quickly became friends.

I asked him if I could come and help him on Saturdays and Sundays and he said that I would always be welcome. I would have to give up my beloved game of cricket for this. I did so gladly because of the opportunity to interact with Muslims, which I enjoyed doing. They would often ask familiar questions or make assertions, such as: "How can God have a son?" or "Surely that Bible of yours is corrupted!" As my background made me well-versed in both the Quran and the Bible, I had interesting and sometimes profound conversations with the passersby, including the opportunity of telling them about the Christian faith. This made the weekends more meaningful and fulfilling for me.

My time at Bible school was an amazing experience! I was learning much regarding "Personal Prayer" and "Intimate Contact with God." And, on one of those days, I learned an important lesson about "Giving" or rather about "Giving and Receiving." This was in response to the text from Luke 6:38, **"Give, and it will be given to you. A good**

measure, pressed down, shaken together and running over, will be poured into your lap." I had only 2,000 rupees in my possession with many items to pay for here, much more than I currently possessed. When the basket for an offering was passed among the students, however, the Lord convicted me to put in 1,000 rupees, and I did it with all my heart for the Lord. Now, I had only 1,000 rupees left and had to work out how to survive with that. But God was faithful! What He promised, He did. A pastor visiting our school as a guest teacher for a few days gave me a gift of 2,000 rupees! A week later, another teacher paid all my school fees for me! Miraculous! I had learned my lesson. What was important was to give generously under the guidance of the Holy Spirit.

Furthermore, here I learned how to share the good news with other people in personal conversations as well as diverse ways to evangelize. Here, I became passionate about spreading the gospel. Also, the close and loving bond with students and teachers felt especially good. Here I was having *"the very best time of my life,"* very special and very precious.

· CHAPTER 9 ·

Outreach

After three months of intensive training, we then went on a mission trip. We called these two-month activities *"outreach."* This was part of our training. We now had to put what we had learned into practice. For this purpose, we were divided into separate groups. Our group consisted of seven people: one male leader, one female leader, and five students, one of whom was a girl. We were a mixed group, coming from many different regions of Pakistan, which made working together extra interesting for us. My team was tasked with heading to another region, where we would visit eight separate places over the next two months.

On the day of our departure, everyone packed his or her backpack with four sets of clothes, one pair of shoes, and personal care items, plus a Bible and a pen for writing. We could take little else with us, so we had to make do with what we had during our two-month trek.

We departed by bus from our high mountain and arrived in the valley via endless curves and hairpin bends. Here, we were immediately confronted with the tremendous heat, which always prevailed in the lower regions of Pakistan around this time of year. A temperature of 45 degrees Celsius was no exception.

Our first destination was a big city. From the moment we stepped off the bus in this place, we heard the passengers speaking only a language that we, except for one of our team members, did not understand at all. We were the only ones speaking Urdu on the bus during the trip. Still, this unknown local language fascinated me, and I tried to catch a few words while listening. I was particularly interested because I had often heard people say that the language of this region was exceedingly difficult to learn. Fortunately, most Christians in this part of Pakistan also spoke Urdu, making it easy for us to be understood.

Our first mission stop was the aforementioned city, from which we would later continue traveling to many other places. In each place where we stayed for missionary work, we were guests of the pastor of a church, but occasionally other Christian families. They provided us with food and a place to sleep during our stay. We visited many homes with families and had frequent opportunities to bring God's Word to people I had never met before. The children received our attention as well and we organized fun meetings for them. I did this work with immense pleasure.

We also went out on the streets and visited markets, stores, and gas stations and handed out brochures and leaflets to anyone who would take them. This kind of work enabled us to talk to many people. Muslims also approached us with many questions and wanted to talk about the differences between their faith and the Christian faith. So, we had numerous opportunities to witness. This filled me with extreme joy. God put a passion in my heart to tell Muslims about my faith. They needed to know the truth!

We moved on and visited many more places in the province assigned to us. We frequently had opportunities to speak with "Christians" who did not have a personal relationship with Jesus. Often, they only knew that they were Christians because their parents and grandparents were. We were able to show them the way, how they could come to a personal faith in Jesus, and receive assurance of the forgiveness of their sins and eternal life. We often prayed with them and helped them take that step.

God used us in various ways. And what made me especially happy was the fact that I could see that I too was an instrument in God's hand and that He used me. I could tell several stories about this, but I will limit myself to just one event.

We were hosting a big outdoor meeting in the evening on a certain day and invited many people to join us. My personal coach approached me and said, "Matthew, tonight it's your turn to bring God's Word!" Frankly, I was a little startled by this and thought to myself, *"Who am I to bring God's message to the people tonight?"* My leader, however, stood firm, despite my opposition, and said I was the best one to do it. And if I indeed could not accomplish it that night or suddenly did not know how to continue, he would come to my aid and take over. But I had to try. So, I found a quiet place and asked my Lord and Savior for a suitable text from the Bible. I tried to prepare as best I could, and by intense prayer placed myself and my message in the Lord's hands.

Evening arrived and I was quite nervous. After a time of worship with music and singing, it was my turn to make my way to the open-air stage we had built. There were more than two hundred people in attendance! They were all sitting on the floor, ready to listen to the message. It was the first time in my life that I had to address so many people. But once I started, God suddenly released all the tension in me. The Holy Spirit gave me the boldness to make God's way known to the people. At the end of my speech, I asked if there might be someone who wanted to dedicate his or her life to Jesus tonight. That person should stand up and our team members would come and pray with him or her. After a short prayer, I opened my eyes and amazement overwhelmed me! About sixty people had stood up to accept Jesus! We prayed with all those people and then had personal conversations with them about following Jesus.

I was so grateful that during this time of intensive service, which also involved indescribable hardships, God showed me that He wanted to use me. And I could only say, "Lord, here I am! I am completely at Your disposal."

After this time of outreach, we returned to our Bible school, where we met all the other teams who had also returned from their field trips. Four full days had been set aside for the members of each team to individually share their experiences and testimonies. The leaders and teachers listened with great interest to the mighty work God had done through all these young students.

Then came the big day for the festive graduation ceremony. I too was proud to receive my diploma. It was a precious moment for me to be able to hold this document in my hands after five months of hard work and learning. It gave me the feeling that I was now a true follower of Jesus.

• CHAPTER 10 •

Calling

ONCE BACK HOME FROM the Bible school, my church's youth group arranged a lovely welcome party for me. On that evening, I was the center of attention and had much to tell. But then life became ordinary again, just like before: working daily in the studio with my boss, in my free time attending the youth meetings, evangelizing and encouraging believers with God's Word.

Three months later, I unexpectedly received a phone call from the leadership of the Bible school. The leader told me that my personality had not gone unnoticed by them during my training. And he continued, "We have seen your great love for God and your passion for Jesus. This made us think. So, we wondered if it would be a good idea for you to come and work with us. Please pray about it and ask God's guidance in this and if this is His plan for you. We will also pray about it and ask God's guidance." I put down the phone and had to process the conversation I just had. This was unbelievable!

I brought this request to the Lord in my personal prayer and asked Him if this was His plan for me. Of course, I also shared this possible new challenge with the youth of my church and my other friends, and certainly also with my pastor. He would also pray about this for God's guidance. But since the request from the Bible school was for me to do volunteer work, the opinion of my friends was divided. Some advised me to go, others discouraged me, arguing, "How are you going to earn a living? Who is going to take care of you? After all, you will have no income."

After much prayer, especially on the part of my pastor, we spoke about it and he said, "YOU MUST GO! I think the Lord is calling you and, who knows, one day you may become a leader!" I saw his face brighten as he spoke these words to me. He had an almost supernatural aura about him and spoke with authority. I recognized a special power in his words and experienced this very moment as a personal calling from God. After this conversation, we continued with prayer, and I then called the leadership of the Bible school to tell them I accepted their offer. "You can count on me!"

A few weeks later, I packed all the possessions I thought I would need as I walked a new road with the Lord. For the second time in my life, I had no idea of what my future would look like as I took the first step in obedience. Once again, I traveled to the city from where you can see the mountains in the distance, but this time not to change to another bus but to join the team of co-workers. During that trip, I particularly experienced the peace and nearness of the Lord. Joy filled me as I reflected on how wonderfully God was leading my life. When

I traveled in this direction for the first time, I went to *learn.* Now I made this trip anew to *serve*. Upon arrival in the city, I was welcomed by the team and allowed to live with a family for the time being.

A few days after that, I met the staff members. Their proposal was to go to the Bible school with them, but this time as a volunteer worker during the education and training of the new students who signed up for this. I attended another training course with four others, this time to *lead*. It was a professional "staff training course," where we learned, among other things, how to deal with and guide the new students. We also discussed correcting and counseling the students in detail. After this intensive and very instructive training course, we all packed our bags and left for our destination high in the mountains, where we made all the preparations to receive and accommodate the new batch of students. For us, this meant that we also had to roll up our sleeves. Everything was ready for the new students just in time.

During the months of training and teaching the students, the staff members came to the decision during one of their meetings to add several "full-time pioneers" as staff members to their team. They could then lead the work in the different cities and regions of Pakistan. To my great surprise, they also chose me. I was immediately reminded of my pastor's apparently prophetic statement, *"YOU MUST GO! I think the Lord is calling you and, who knows, **one day you may become a 'leader.'**"*

Quite something, indeed! Receiving responsibility and leading pioneering work in other cities and remote places! We would receive a small basic monthly stipend with which we would have to survive. For the remainder, we would have to trust our God that He would provide.

There was another special moment during the time I guided students in their studies. I suddenly saw the girl whom I thought may become my future wife! She was one of the new students, but she was not on the team that I supervised. I did not know her at all and only saw her occasionally from a distance. When she looked in my direction, my heart began to beat faster. One of those inexplicable things in life!

A few months later, the students were able to successfully complete their studies and two months of practice in the form of outreach followed. Yes, outreach was familiar to me when I was a student myself. Now, I had the opportunity for outreach again, but this time as a "leader." I was now in charge of a group of young people who wanted to learn to serve Jesus among the people.

The Lord greatly blessed us. People were being converted and baptized. We were reaching curious Muslims and Hindus with the message of God's love. We also had opportunities to encourage people with God's Word in various house meetings. In addition, we reached many children with the gospel by organizing special meetings for them. It was a very blessed outreach but accompanied by many hardships. That was part of the cost if you want to reach people with the gospel.

With hearts filled with joy, we returned from the outreach and met with all the other teams. There were several days of meetings, where each group would report in detail about their work and experiences and how God had been able to use them.

And yes, there she was again! The lovely girl who did outreach on another team. During these days she kept popping into my mind, and during the meetings her eyes kept going in my direction. I was distraught and did not know what to do. I had no parents who could mediate according to Pakistani tradition. However, I did start praying about it and asked God if it was His will.

Then something very unusual happened on the last day of our stay. This lovely girl came up to me during a break and asked if she could tell me something. With a pounding heart and quite fazed, I said, "Go ahead!" And then suddenly, she said, "Will you marry me?" I was shocked! I did not expect this! And frankly, I would not have had the courage to ask her. I forced myself to control my feelings and tried to appear as calm as possible. Then I told her that I would give her my answer later.

I wanted to talk to my leaders about this first. And most importantly, I wanted to pray about this and ask God for His guidance. I didn't give her any answer at that moment. We exchanged phone numbers and then "Saima" walked back to the other girls, her fellow students.

After the graduation ceremony, Saima returned home to her family like all the other students. I did not have a home! So, I packed my things and returned to our headquarters in the valley to resume my work there.

• CHAPTER 11 •

Mistrust and Discrimination

THE WORK AT THE headquarters kept me quite busy over the weeks that followed. Early every morning, I first sought personal contact with my God through prayer and reading His Word. Invariably, the name *Saima* came into my personal prayers. We occasionally sent each other short messages on our cell phones. That was our only contact.

After four weeks, I finally found the courage to talk to my supervisors. I told them about Saima and asked them what they thought about my marrying her. Their response was, "Oh, that's great! Yes, Saima would certainly be a good woman for you, if you could marry her. But then we must talk to her family." I said that I agreed to do whatever they deemed necessary in this matter.

Thus, a few days later, one of my leaders went to visit Saima's parents who were devout Christians. When they heard that this was a marriage proposal for their daughter, they called the whole family together. Who was this young man who was interested in their daughter? And what kind of family would she end up in? These were important questions in Pakistan in response to a marriage proposal!

Yes, their daughter recently successfully completed training at the Bible school. And they were quite proud of that. But why was the leader the one presenting a marriage proposal? Surely the young man's father should do that. They soon had their answers.

Meanwhile, Saima's mother placed a tray with cups steaming with original Pakistani tea on the small coffee table, quite a strong brew, prepared beforehand with milk and sugar. Then, this leader, who was the head of all the staff, told the family why he had come there with a marriage proposal. He told them that the young man in question was a very devout Christian, but with an Islamic background. So, he was a converted Muslim. He was known by the name *"Matthew,"* but his real name was Salman Ahmed.

An uncomfortable silence followed. No one seemed happy with this. More questions came up about his parents and relatives. And then they learned the sad story. Because of his conversion from Islam to Christianity, which was strictly forbidden in Pakistan, his entire family had turned against him. Out of shame over this, they even tried to kill him. And because of the threat of a second attempt on his life, he had to flee and go into hiding.

The relatives of Saima's father clearly expressed their opposition to this marriage and strongly advised against it. Saima's parents adopted a somewhat milder attitude, but also expressed their concerns. In the end, the leader solemnly promised them that he would personally take responsibility for Saima should she ever get into trouble because of the marriage to "Matthew," which of course he absolutely did not expect.

The leader's commitment to protect Saima somewhat reassured her parents. Finally, albeit reluctantly, they gave their consent. In the meantime, the rest of the family slowly came around and a date was set for the official engagement.

I was anxiously awaiting the return of our highly esteemed leader. I was very curious about the outcome and wanted to know all the details. And yes, there it was again, the distrust of Christians towards me, an ex-Muslim. I unfortunately encountered this form of discrimination on many occasions. It was uncertain if Saima's family would ever truly accept me. But this doubt did not hit me that hard this time. After all, this was about the courting of a girl, with whom I was madly in love. All that mattered to me was that they finally gave their consent. The way it happened did not matter so much anymore.

I could not contain my joy and expressed my gratitude to my leader, who was able to successfully accomplish this challenging task with the help of our God. Even greater was my gratitude to my Savior Jesus Christ who, by His Holy Spirit, guided hearts and had finally brought this engagement to fruition. Glory be to His Name!

• CHAPTER 12 •

Persecution

After the official engagement, Saima and I did not meet again until our wedding, fifteen months later. During this time of waiting, Saima had the opportunity to volunteer at the Bible school. And I returned to my place of work at the headquarters of our organization in the valley. Saima and I spoke to each other only occasionally by phone. Pakistani customs did not give us the opportunity to become better acquainted with each other. That would have to happen after the wedding!

* * *

Since my conversion, I had an unsolvable problem. Every Pakistani identity card or passport identifies the holder's religion. My identity card showed that I was Muslim. And since Pakistani law strictly forbids a Muslim to become a Christian, it was also not possible to change this in your ID. So, after all the years of being a follower of Jesus Christ, I was still a Muslim according to my ID. And if the police, during a check, found me in the company of Christians, I would have some serious explaining to do! I could count on a response of brute force.

One evening, fourteen of us gathered for prayer at our headquarters. Suddenly, a group of police officers interrupted our prayers by storming in, with their automatic weapons pointed at us! We were all terribly frightened. What was going on? With what false accusations have Muslim neighbors again "blackballed" us to the government? Asking "why?" and "for what reason?" was not an option. They gave us a crude indication that they were the only ones asking questions. They randomly grabbed five people from the group. Apparently, they did not have enough room in their two vehicles as they had not expected such a large group.

I was one of them whom they grabbed firmly. "Show your ID!" they commanded. With trembling hands and a quick prayer to my God, I pulled out my ID card. Under the "religion" section it read *"Muslim"* in clear letters. Outraged, they shouted at me, "You are a Muslim! What are you doing here?" I received hard blows to my face and head, while they scolded me with all sorts of filthy words.

Meanwhile, among the five arrested, they discovered another ex-Muslim! He received the same "treatment" as me. The other three were registered as "Christians" and were taken away somewhat more quietly.

The police confiscated my cell phone as they pushed me into the police jeep. On the way to the station, they fired all sorts of questions at us. Upon arrival, we were all taken into a small room. The police did not allow us to speak to each other and there was constant surveillance.

Then the endless interrogation began. Hours later, the police released the three Christians. But both of us with Muslim IDs had to stay. The interrogation continued all night, hour after hour, without food or water, just questions and heavy accusations, which made no sense. The police threatened us with long-term incarceration.

They wanted to know what we were doing in the headquarters of this Christian organization. "You are Muslim!" they shouted at us. "What are you doing in this place?" My brain anxiously searched for an answer acceptable to them. If I told the truth, they may even kill me! Finally, I said that we were only there as students to learn English and take computer classes. I tried to convince them we were not there for any other reason.

For a moment it seemed they were satisfied with this explanation. But then the detective cast another glance at my ID and said: "You are not from here. You are from another region. Why have you come all the way here for these classes? Surely you can take them in your city of birth?"

"Yes, but there I could not find work anywhere and here I can" was my quick reply.

After a brief consultation, the police informed us that our presence in this place and the neighboring city was undesirable. They demanded that we leave as soon as possible and return to where we came from. "We never want to see you here again!" they added, to make it clear to us that they meant business. And then we were set free.

The sun was just beginning to rise as we made our way back to the place where people had been praying for us all night. We were hungry but mostly thirsty. After a little refreshment, we had to give an account. All the leaders were genuinely concerned about our situation and advised us to leave this region for the time being for security reasons.

• CHAPTER 13 •

Nowhere to Stay

I HAD TO LEAVE this city, otherwise the police would lock me up. But where should I go? The authorities wanted me to return to my birth city, but I had fled from there just a few years ago. My relatives, who were all fanatical Muslims, wanted to kill me because I converted to Jesus Christ. I did not feel safe there. If they found out that I was in their city, then my life would be in great danger.

But my Christian friends advised me, nevertheless, to really go to my city of birth now, even if only for a brief time. After all, I had been told to do so by the police. But where would I find safe lodging in that big city?

I remembered that, during the time I taught at the Bible school, there were also two girl students from my home city. Once, when their mother had come to visit them, I started a conversation with her, and as we parted, she said to me, "If you ever need help, you are always welcome to come to us." And she gave me their address.

"Maybe this was an option," I thought. It was a huge city. If I stayed far enough away from the neighborhood where my family lived, they would not easily discover me. The neighborhood where this Christian family lived did seem suitable for a brief period. So, I left and after a long journey I arrived at their doorstep. I was warmly welcomed and stayed there for a whole month.

For my safety, it did not seem wise to stay in this place any longer. Besides, I did not have much to do here. So, I packed my backpack again and left. Since I had been following Jesus, this had become my regular living pattern. But out of love for Him I was willing to endure all this. Jesus also had no fixed abode and often did not know where to lay His head at night. After all, I was a follower of Him. This way of life was apparently part of it.

Thankfully, another fellow staff member invited me to come and stay with him for the time being. The city where he lived and worked for Jesus is not that big. As his place of residence was close to the border with Afghanistan, however, it was not exactly the safest environment since a Taliban fighter could be your neighbor. But I took my chances and began my journey there. Where else could I go?

After a train trip of many exhausting hours and then several more hours on a crowded bus, I reached my destination. Here, I really felt like a stranger because I could not understand anything the people around me were saying. Nobody here seemed to understand or speak Urdu. Thankfully, after a few moments, I discovered my friend among the huge crowd of people. He guided me safely to his house.

We had much to share with each other, but also went out together regularly, to serve our Lord and Savior and encourage Christians in this dangerous region. Since it was not safe for me to stay here either, a month later I packed my backpack again with my few belongings.

I could no longer find a place to stay except where the police had abused me more than two months before. I would have to return there, even though my presence in this place was unwanted by the police. I had been invited to stay with a dear family there for the time being. So, I took my chances, hoping not to be caught and praying daily for supernatural protection. The gentleman of the house was the pastor of a congregation, and he asked me to assist him in his work. I did this with immense pleasure and dedication. I could stay longer with this family. Therefore,

I would not leave this place until the dawn of my wedding celebration days with Saima.

• CHAPTER 14 •

On the Run Again

FINALLY, THE TIME HAD come. I was to marry the girl of my dreams! As Pakistani tradition dictates, our wedding celebration lasted for three days. We enjoyed all the attention, the various ceremonies, and the good food. At the end of all the festivities, we were taken to a nice hotel for our first wedding night. The following six days we stayed at my in-laws' house.

Meanwhile, a new group of students from the Bible school had successfully completed their training and now had to do outreach for two months. Despite being newly married, I was told that, as a staff member, I had to lead one of the outreach teams. So, no "honeymoon"! No privacy! We spent entire days on the road taking the gospel to remote places. We spent many nights in various places with hospitable Christians, the young men in one dormitory and the young women in another.

For Saima and me, these were two trying months, but the Lord helped us to persevere and accomplish our work with joy, dedication, and much blessing. Back at the Bible school, the evaluation of the outreach took place, followed by the graduation ceremony and festive conclusion. After these blessed days, we saw one student after another leaving with their baggage. They were all going home. How Saima and I would also like to go home! But we did not have a home! Since following Jesus, I had never had a "home." My marriage to Saima had not changed that either.

* * *

Being a pioneer staff member, Saima and I were deployed to a town in another region to serve our God there. It was considered a very unsafe area. Unfortunately, the people there did not speak Urdu either. And so, in the beginning, we had great difficulty making ourselves understood. But Saima had the brilliant idea of teaching the children Urdu at school as this was the official and most widely spoken language in Pakistan. The children would need it in the future for further education and possible training.

Upon our arrival at this new location, we were given a small room. There we settled in for the next twelve months. There was little furniture in it, but we made do.

Saima taught at our small elementary school. Since there was no other school in the wider area, many students came from Muslim families. I instructed adults in Arabic and English. My students were also mostly Muslim and thus interested in the Arabic language.

In Pakistan, it was strictly forbidden to preach the gospel to Muslims. By offering them education, we had the opportunity to grow closer to them and gain their trust. Then, personal conversations naturally developed, including religious matters and the difference between Islam and Christianity. And so the question naturally arose, *"What is truth?"*

The twelve months of our service in this region had not yet passed. Suddenly, in the middle of the night, there was a violent knock on our room door. We heard our coworkers shouting fearfully, "Get up quickly!" Sleep-deprived, we crawled out of bed and opened the door. "You have to get out of here!" we heard our coworkers say. From what they said we understood it to be about our safety.

We rubbed the sleep out of our eyes, gathered the essentials, and quickly packed them in our bags. After a brief prayer for protection and a warm goodbye, we made our way to the bus stop while it was still dark so no one would see us. We waited at the bus stop until the very first bus arrived very early in the morning. We boarded and left this area unnoticed.

Our staff had been tipped off by loyal neighbors that a police raid was expected the next day. Rumors had spread about us during the last few days that we were only using the school and all the other teaching we did as a cover. We were not teaching but trying to convert people to the Christian faith.

This also explained why in recent days fewer and fewer children appeared at our school. It seemed that parents had kept their children at home under pressure from the Imam. This incited local Muslims to demand that the police investigate.

It would not end well for me if they found out I was a converted Muslim. The police always asked for your ID at such an investigation. And even after my marriage to Saima, who was registered as a Christian, my ID still stated that I was Muslim. The only way to stay out of their hands was to disappear from this place as soon as possible.

The raid did indeed take place that morning, but because the other employees were "generation Christians" and nothing else was found indicating "criminal offenses," they left them alone. Thankfully, I escaped torture and perhaps even death at the cruel hands of the police just in time. I was on the run again, but this time together with my brave wife, Saima.

• CHAPTER 15 •

Future Prospects

AFTER A LENGTHY TRIP, we arrived tired and dejected at our headquarters, where accommodation was quickly arranged for us. We were assigned a room, where we unpacked the few belongings we were able to take with us in our hasty departure. There was a mattress on the floor where we could catch up on our lack of sleep. And we did. This mattress would be our sleeping place for a long time to come. However, most important to us was safety. For now, we had that here.

We made ourselves useful where we could and participated in all staff meetings. A new national program for the coming months was being prepared. To our great relief, Saima and I would not be sent to such a dangerous area again but would be permanent staff members at the Bible school. I would teach certain subjects there, including about Islam and how to engage in conversation with our Muslim neighbors and friends.

In addition, Saima and I would supervise the students and do practical and organizational work as needed. I would supervise the kitchen and oversee the preparation of meals for sixty people. Purchasing food for all these meals was also entrusted to me.

Occasionally, Saima and I had the opportunity to accompany foreign guests on their missions and function as interpreters during their frequent speaking engagements. It was a blessed ministry that gave us great satisfaction.

Finally, the two months of outreach were on the horizon again. This time I would go alone. I had to leave my beloved wife with her parents for that period. She was expecting our first baby and would not be able to manage the hard life full of inconveniences during my mission trips with the students.

I was quite worried about our future! How would we cope with raising a child who had no fixed abode? I turned my concern into a prayer to the God who could do everything. He was undoubtedly able to provide a small home where our child could be born and grow up in a safe environment.

The personal sponsorship we received monthly from our organization was far too little to rent a home. But our Almighty God would provide a solution. I had that trust and continued to pray intensely for this.

Finally, the time of outreach and all the closing festivities was over, and I was back at headquarters. Saima was still with her parents in another city, far away. I felt lonely without her and missed her very much. But how could I bring her here if I could not even offer her a decent bed?

But God be praised! He is miraculous! Once again, He came through just in time with the answer to our prayers. Our God provided new sponsors so that I was now able to rent a modest home in a Christian neighborhood. After searching for a while, I found a suitable space with God's help.

The Lord also blessed us with additional gifts so that I could purchase a spacious bed with a good mattress. In Pakistan, a bed with mattress served not only to sleep on but was also the centerpiece of homelife. In addition, it provided seating for us and any guests. Moreover, with a clean tablecloth underneath, food was served in the middle of the large family bed. One then sat with legs folded at the head and foot end to eat.

All the work, which in Western countries was normally done in the living room or at a writing desk, was done here on the bed by poorer families. And at night the entire family slept on this bed. Thus, our bed would have many purposes. I was grateful to my dear friends, who made it possible to purchase not only a spacious bed, but also a refrigerator and a simple stove. I felt like royalty.

Our "cottage" was finally ready, so I could now fetch Saima! What a joy to see each other again after more than three months! For the first time in our marriage, we had a place which we could call *"home."* We enjoyed the privacy, which you rarely have in Pakistan.

A few months later, our *"gift from God"* was born vigorous and healthy. It was a boy! We named him Joshua and were intensely happy with him. We received many calls from friends, neighbors, and people from our church. All came to congratulate us on the birth of our son and expressed their wishes of blessing on the young life our God had entrusted to us.

Excited, I went to the City Office, to declare the birth of our son and register him as a "Christian." The official looked at my papers and those of the mother and said, "Sir, that is not possible! You are registered as a 'Muslim,' so your son will also be registered as a 'Muslim.'"

"But the mother is Christian" was my counterargument. "That is not our concern," said the employee at the counter. "This is the law! The children always receive the identity of the father, including the religion."

Totally defeated and deeply saddened, I went home. I had not yet registered the birth. Would I have to saddle my children with the same fate that I had to go through life with? Would our son be beaten too in his later life by the police or the military if they discovered him with his Muslim ID among the Christians? Would he too have to risk being jailed for following Jesus? I could not bear this thought!

Over the next few days and months, I would be checking all the authorities and trying to find out if there were any loopholes in the law that might offer a way for my little boy to register as a Christian. But the problem in my country is that no one wants to cooperate.

***

All Christians in Pakistan struggle! But if you dare to become a Christian as a Muslim, **the price you pay can be very high!**

Still, I am determined to continue following Jesus. I will serve Him with all my heart, despite all the pressures, all the beatings and tortures, that I have had to endure so far. I have no idea what lies ahead for me and our young family. But I keep in mind that Jesus paid a much higher price to redeem us from our sins. He is worth every sacrifice!

I want to conclude my testimony with the well-known English song, which has been sung with abandon by thousands of Christians all over the world, but often without grasping the depth and possible consequences. I am one of your Christian brothers who has the privilege of suffering and, if necessary, dying for Jesus. My suffering has given this song a much deeper meaning for me.

I HAVE DECIDED TO FOLLOW JESUS!

NO TURNING BACK! NO TURNING BACK!

THE WORLD BEHIND ME—THE CROSS BEFORE ME.

NO TURNING BACK! NO TURNING BACK!

THOUGH NONE GO WITH ME—STILL I WILL FOLLOW.

NO TURNING BACK! NO TURNING BACK!

• CHAPTER 16 •

Six Years Later

SO MUCH HAPPENED OVER the next six years! God is good, infinitely good! And He takes care of His children. Thankfully, nomadic life is over for Salman and Saima. They no longer must move from one place to another. They also no longer need to worry every month about how to pay the rent for a small primitive house with all kinds of defects.

With the help of Saima's family and faithful Christian friends, Salman managed to buy a small piece of land and some building materials. There, he and his Pakistani friends were able to build a small house, which he can call his own. The house is large enough to receive relatives or friends. However, when it comes to contacts with *"seekers"* or newly converted followers of Jesus, he meets them in neutral outdoor places, such as parks. This is safer for Salman and for the visitors.

* * *

Meanwhile, God has also blessed their marriage with a second son, Emmanuel. He is very active and mischievous. Much to the family's enjoyment, he is trying to talk now. Joshua is already going to school and doing very well. In addition to reading, writing, and math, he is learning English and taking group keyboard lessons at a worship academy. He really enjoys playing keyboard and practices at home every day. In addition, he enjoys listening to worship music. He is also interested in soccer and enjoys attending the local Sunday school and listening to Bible stories.

As described earlier, it was impossible to register Joshua as a Christian after his birth. According to Pakistani law, a child is always given the identity of the father, including religion. And since it is forbidden for a Muslim to change religion, it is also impossible to do so in Salman's official documents. In Pakistan, every identity card or passport also indicates the religion. This would mean that all his children will be registered as Muslims with all the unpleasant consequences, which he has had to experience so many times himself.

After a long and uncertain journey through multiple administrative corridors – reaching even the highest tiers of authority – and despite personal risk at every turn, no hopeful outcome seemed to emerge. Yet, in the silence that often follows struggle, a subtle opening appeared. The children could now be identified according to their spiritual heritage.

However this came with a personal cost: They could not formally carry the name that linked them to their lineage. Their identities were simplified, defined by singular names without the traditional continuity. This quiet adjustment, though heavy, brings with it a future possibility. Perhaps one day, their own children will reclaim those names as a family legacy. Remarkably, the system does allow for such a restoration in the next generation.

As you have read, Salman's father, his uncle, and his brother-in-law tried to kill him when they discovered that he had become a Christian. Salman was willing to die for Jesus. But God wanted him to live! Therefore, the "revenge of honor" had failed. He had to flee and adopt another name far from home. Otherwise, he could still be killed. Since then, there has been no contact with his family. This filled him with great sadness. He realized all too well that, despite their strict religiosity, his relatives would be lost to him forever. And that hurt. He prayed fervently for them for many years, cherishing the hope that one day they too would become followers of Jesus.

One day the shocking news that his father had died reached him through friends. What should he do? Should he undertake the distant journey to bury his father? The other family members, who threatened him with death, would all be there! All sorts of things went through his mind. Did Papa really die? Could it be a trap to lure him home to kill him? A good Christian friend from that same region finally confirmed that the news was true.

Meanwhile, he spoke to his wife Saima about this, and together they prayed fervently to God for guidance. There was not much time for reflection. Salman had the feeling that he had to go. And his brave wife said, with great decisiveness, "I'll go with you, and we'll take Joshua too." They were aware that this venture involved a great risk, and no one knew how it would turn out.

Therefore, he also confided in some close friends and asked for prayer. A domestic flight was quickly booked, and they left with an attitude of "***If I die, I die!***" You can find this statement in a similar situation in

Esther 4:16b of the Bible. With great fervor, friends appealed to our Savior, Jesus Christ, throughout the day! It became an incredibly tense day for those who prayed and even more so for Salman and Saima.

After a long time of expectancy, we heard that their trip to Salman's home was going well so far. At least his eldest sister was happy to see him again after so many years. The men in the family, however, ignored him and he felt hatred and rejection. So, Salman wisely chose not to spend the night with his family.

But he did something else that surely made a big impression on them. As the only son of the deceased, he took charge of the funeral preparations and paid all the expenses. It would be a simple funeral, as prescribed by Islam. He also paid to feed all the guests. This commanded respect and probably some surprise. His eldest sister was very grateful for his unexpected help. But the men involved in the failed murder attempt, referred to as an *"honor killing,"* did not hide their hatred. Consequently, they did not exchange a single word with him.

Salman remained in his hometown for several more days, visiting his eldest sister and her young adult children every day. By doing so, he hoped to show a little more of his love and interest in them and to share something about his faith with them. He looks forward to the day when they too will become followers of Jesus Christ. The fire in his heart, lit by God to reach *"his people"* with the gospel, continues to burn unabated! His wife Saima is proud of him and vigorously supports him in her prayers.

Every morning, she wakes Joshua and dresses him so Salman can take him to school on the motorcycle. He also picks him up later in the day. He takes care of all other necessary rides because the motorcycle is their only means of transportation. In Pakistan, you often see whole families riding on one motorcycle. So, the four of them often ride the motorcycle in the middle of heavy traffic with cars, trucks, and buses and rely on God's protection.

While Saima does the housework, provides meals, and looks after their youngest, Salman continues tirelessly to make tentative contacts with interested or seeking Muslims. They call these people *"persons of peace."* Each evening, they spend extensive time praying together for all things.

Through the prophets of the Quran, he shows that Jesus is much more than a prophet, as Islam teaches. This approach, however, through personal contacts, is time-consuming. One day he received a clear vision from God on how it could also be done more effectively.

These are Salman's own words: "None of us would dispute that the advent of the mobile phone has changed the world. This change has taken a little longer to reach Pakistan.

But now it has happened, and it has made a great impact.

"Thousands of Pakistanis have discovered the Internet as a new source of truth. My neighbors are 'googling' questions, which they would never dare to discuss with their friends, for fear of vehement religious reactions and condemnation. The Internet, especially social media, is becoming our marketplace for new ideas.

"It has been about two years since I was given the vision for 'online outreach.' Through social media, I might offer a structured online course. Of course, I will also continue my other means of personal evangelism. In the meantime, I have already started to scatter the gospel seed abundantly through online advertisements. But, as of now, I will mainly be focusing on preparations for the online Bible classes through social media. The course will be offered at no cost to interested Pakistanis. This course is designed for those who are sincerely curious about life's deeper questions. The course is grounded in a shared spiritual heritage, drawing from narratives and figures that many people in our context already revere and recognize. This approach builds on common ground, inviting deeper reflections without confrontation.

"What is the purpose of all this? '**Pakistanis Meet Jesus.**' Thus, social media open an avenue for us to identify interested people. And the online classes will help students discover 'the truth.' But it will also help *us* find the serious seekers. Because if someone from the religious majority makes the effort to study all my online classes to the end, I would like to meet that person! Such a person has shown real hunger and has spared no effort to find out the truth. I would like to know them personally and share with them the truth, which can change people's lives. We will then organize 'face-to-face follow-up' with whomever we can."

A ministry friend recently commented, "This strategy of using the Internet to identify serious seekers and then connect them with us on the ground . . . has been better for us than having one hundred cups of tea with our neighbors, hoping that one of them will be interested in Jesus."

Of course, a beautiful dream, or a grandiose idea, must become a reality. Salman started working on this. He began to develop studies in Urdu, the official language in Pakistan, a work of many months. These studies were designed to arouse the interest of seeking Muslims. He even opened a special website for this purpose.

Salman says that more than a thousand people have logged into this site. This they can do late at night without anyone in their family being aware of it. The website works and many seekers have already secretly completed full courses online. Salman explains, "With this online ministry, I reach many people but must spend many hours at the computer every day to do so. I also provide 'training by appointment' in neutral outdoor locations such as parks. Each time we meet at a different location, just as described in the Bible's book of Acts. This protects my own safety as well as the visitors. Thus, at these blessed meetings, I can quote from the Bible and pray with those attending. At these outdoor 'house church services,' I can give them a New Testament or a Bible if they want. When they ask me if I am a follower of Jesus, I always answer honestly.

"Such church services generally last two hours and are usually held on Saturdays. We then study the Bible together and the visitors learn to pray to Jesus. When they have accepted Jesus, we also baptize them if they request it. Jesus teaches us that true followers of Him must also make other *disciples* (followers) of Jesus. These *MBBs* (Muslim Background Believers) take this command of Jesus very seriously and go in search of a 'person of peace,' someone who seeks and is open-minded. And so our numbers increase!"

God is miraculously at work in a country where it is forbidden to approach Muslims with the gospel, and where a Muslim converting to Christianity is punishable by death. In Romans 1:16, the Apostle Paul says, ***"For I am not ashamed of the gospel, because it is THE POWER OF GOD THAT BRINGS SALVATION to everyone who believes."*** There is no way to stop the gospel of Jesus Christ, even in a strict Islamic country like Pakistan. But it does take courage and, sometimes, casualties.

MBBs avoid martyrdom and persecution as much as possible. So did the first Christians, as described in Acts. The gospel would not spread if all these new MBBs were to die as martyrs, no matter how brave and admirable that would be. Even though Salman was willing to die for Jesus, God wanted him to live. And surely Jesus also wants many of those precious souls, who found Him after long searching, to live. Then they can grow in faith and prudently multiply. So, the advice of Salman and his team is, "Don't tell your family! It's only about 'You and Jesus—Jesus and you' now."

Of course, close relatives, such as the spouses, children, or parents of these converts, may discover that MBBs are engaged in unauthorized "sleuthing" or reading "the forbidden book." This can trigger violent confrontations and even threats! In such situations, they face persecution anyway. There are indeed reports of heated discussions and resulting conflicts of serious marital problems and reproaches. The risk of persecution always exists! But family members may themselves become curious. God is at work in all sorts of ways! Salman is developing support courses to encourage and help these MBBs deal with this.

***

When the conflicts broke out and a wave of instability swept across the region, many vulnerable families crossed into safer territory, weak, weary and desperate. They walked for days without food, water or proper shelter. Some collapsed shortly after arriving and for others help came too late.

Moved by compassion, Salman and his team offered help to these families, who often camped under a self-built shelter to escape the hot sun. Here, Salman's team sought them out, wrote down their names, and noted everything they needed. They provided clean drinking water and, where necessary, slightly better shelter. They shopped, especially for food, but also for blankets, pillows, medicine, and other personal needs. They provided all that for them, as well as the gospel!

For six months they helped and guided these families. New people kept coming until there were about fifty families! But amazingly, almost half of these families became followers of Jesus! They asked to be baptized and then received teaching and training. The people grew in faith and over time some families were even sent out to evangelize!

Meanwhile, some of them formed their own churches. Others started looking for "persons of peace," and so the multiplication started, even among these newly converted believers.

***

When asked to talk about the future, Salman says enthusiastically, "Yes, I have a dream! It's more than a dream. It is an expectation! Because the work that we do here, by grace, is not our work, but the work of the Holy Spirit who is in us and works through us. In the future, many people from the religious majority will come to faith. They will follow Jesus and tell others about Him. I long to see those to whom 'discipleship' has been taught not merely remain students, but also seek out others and help them become followers of Jesus. All to greatly increase the footprint of Christianity. I believe that before I die, I will witness at least seven generations of people who have found the way to Jesus!

"I pray that God's Holy Spirit will accomplish a 'movement of discipleship,' multiplying by sharing with seekers, again and again. I long to see this movement set in motion, a movement that begins with one disciple and eventually reaches thousands of seekers. Because there are indeed many! Thus, we will witness a movement, as described in the book of Revelation, when an innumerable multitude from every tongue and tribe is glorifying Jesus Christ. This is my expectation for the future, my prayer and my passion, for which I live and commit myself."

Postscript

THE GOSPEL IS NOT bound! It cannot be stopped by any authority or power! The book you have just read is proof of that! After all, it is a true story, a report of facts that have taken place and are still taking place now. The gospel is God's saving power, entrusted to us by Jesus Himself. What do we as Western Christians do with it? Or what have we made of it?

Is the text in 1 Timothy 2:3b–4, which speaks about **"God, our Savior, who wants all people to be saved and to come to a knowledge of the truth,"** only intended for a country such as "the Islamic Republic of Pakistan"? Isn't it high time for all Western believers to rise up from our "comfortable Sunday pews" and do something with that saving power of God which He entrusted to all of us? Is it enough to leave it to our fellow Pakistani Christians to be brave and admirable? We may be willing to pray for them and possibly support them financially. This is also needed and will further advance the expansion of God's kingdom on earth.

However, **this story** should motivate us to break out of our comfort zone because Jesus is calling us as well! There are also many "*seekers*" in Western countries. They must be found!

Living in a Western country, we do not normally have to face persecution, abuse, or death because of the gospel. **But should it not cost us something?** We will not be spared hardship and discomfort here either. Jesus says: "***Take up your cross and follow Me!***" Are we "paying the price for following Jesus" in our countries?

May this book challenge and inspire all of us! The "*seekers*" are waiting for us!

Eva Wongsosemito

About the Author

EVA WONGSOSEMITO HAS SERVED the Lord faithfully for many years as a missionary, speaker, teacher, and writer. She and her husband have been married for over 56 years and have three married children and many grand- and great-grandchildren. She was born in a region of East Germany which is now part of Poland. Because she grew up during World War II, she had to flee many times due to war violence. Because of this transient life, she had no roots anywhere and very little education. However, the good Lord gave Eva an inquisitive and retentive brain, and she was able to complete her schooling after the war with good grades. Eva speaks five different languages.

Eva's walk with the Lord began at the age of 18 when she accepted Jesus as her personal Savior through the enthusiastic testimony of several young people. Not long after her conversion, God called her to serve Him in missionary work. She graduated from a Bible college in Switzerland. After learning the Dutch language in the Netherlands, she traveled to Suriname, a former Dutch colony in South America. In this country, she served as a missionary for 40 years and as a pastor's wife for the last 17 years. In response to the immense suffering of children in that country at that time, Eva and her husband added 16 foster children to their family. Eva gave many television interviews in Suriname and the Netherlands and was frequently invited for speaking engagements in the Netherlands, Germany, Pakistan, and Sweden.

After their retirement, Eva and her husband settled in the Netherlands with their five youngest foster children. Eva has continued her speaking ministry. She has also written two books and is working on a third. Eva has a heart for those who are sharing the gospel in difficult circumstances around the world.

www.ingramcontent.com/pod-product-compliance
Lightning Source LLC
Chambersburg PA
CBHW020356170426
43200CB00005B/186